CAMILA

Like Father, Like Son

Hope You Enjoy The Book

Best of Luck

Matt Anthony

Acknowledgments

My thanks for all of the hard work and expertise
contributed by Nathan Williams and Chris Kwiatkowski
in helping me write this book.

For my brother Gerry: You have been with me every stride, and are always at your best when I need you the most.

For Bill Dellinger: Through your coaching, guidance and friendship, we forged an Olympic bond that will last forever.

Like Father, Like Son

by

Matt Centrowitz

with

Nathan Williams and Chris Kwiatkowski

Introduction

I have a unique perspective, having lived through the sport of track and field in three different identities - as an Olympic athlete, a NCAA Division-1 head coach, and a parent to an Olympic athlete. I have personally experienced or witnessed just about every aspect of this sport. My success, and the success of my family, is due to the coaches and teammates who came across my life. I was lucky enough to have encountered each of them at the pinnacle of their craft.

Coach Milt Blatt and Brother John Beilen ushered me into an era of New York City at a time when NY track was the gold standard around the US. Their respective programs at Andrew Jackson High and Power Memorial High set national records and produced Olympic Champions - something that hasn't been duplicated since.

Coaches Fred Dwyer and Frank Gagliano sent Manhattan College bursting onto the national track scene, winning the 1973 NCAA Indoor Track championship in dramatic fashion - with a team full of New York City kids.

And at the University of Oregon, Bill Bowerman was pioneering a legacy of NCAA Champions and Olympians - a legacy which Bill Dellinger was not only a part of (becoming Bowerman's first Olympian in 1956), but would later add to as Oregon's head track coach.

These men were all very different, each with a style quite their own, but they shared a common thread - in order to be successful in such a demanding sport, you need to have fun.

For many people, the process of writing an autobiography is in large part cathartic - to unburden past torments and emotions. But for me, my catharsis was raising a family with three fun-loving children. I wrote this book to help others, with hope that someone reading it might learn something: that it might provide fresh insight to a seasoned coach, motivation to the developing athlete, or a fun perspective for a track parent.

This book is about my time spent in sport and the profound effect it had on me and my family.

This is my story.

"Your body moves always in the present, the dividing line between the past and the future. But your mind is more free. It can think, and is in the present. It can remember, and at once is in the past. It can imagine, and at once is in the future, in its own choice of all the possible futures. Your mind can travel through time!"

CHAPTER ONE: RIO

"Run for gold, nothing else." I told him, "You've worked too hard and have come too far to pick off any other medal. Just go for it. Take that risk. Whatever you do, don't play it safe."

He nodded, fierce determination already cemented on his face, on the eve of the Olympic finals in the 1500m.

Keeping with our tradition, we hashed out pre-race thoughts. Usually our talks centered around tactics, especially dangerous competitors, the reward at the end — at times motivating, other times calming. But for this race, the biggest of both our lives, we focused on one thing: family.

"I'm so proud of you and all of your success on and off the track. You have done something I've wanted to do my whole life — unite our family."

My son, Matthew Centrowitz, was about to run in his second Olympic final. Four years earlier he narrowly missed a bronze medal by less than a twentieth of a second. Now at 26 he was mentally tougher, his preparation at a much higher level, and more importantly, hungrier and more confident than I had ever seen him.

"You're ready, son," I told him as we shook hands. "Go." We said goodnight and parted ways. The next time I would see him was in the Olympic stadium. He looked cool and confident, winking as he gave me a thumbs up from the side of the track. I took my seat and anxiously awaited the race.

As someone who's competed in the Olympics, I knew there's no telling what can happen in a final. That's the interesting thing about an Olympic final in the middle and long distance races. Tactics rule, and the unexpected almost always happens. You just never know how the race will turn out.

Casual fans might think these things are pretty straight-forward. Everybody runs as hard as they can, fastest guy wins. And, sure, for the most part, the guy with elite speed is going to beat the guy that snuck into the final. People who know track, though, know there's a lot more to it. An Olympic final is its own animal. It's not like a race on the European circuit with a rabbit and a bunch of runners trying to set personal records. In an Olympic final, there is no set script. It's an original screenplay that begins writing itself once the gun goes off. At this super elite level, the distance races take on unique characteristics.

2

In championship races , the 1500m unfolds with a different rhythm each time. No human being can run full out for the entire race. There is always this complex calculation of energy, nerve and strategy. The tendency is to hang back, to conserve strength for some vital moment, hoping, betting, praying, that your reserve, your heart, will be bigger than your opponent's. There is drama and gamesmanship, psychological warfare and risky jockeying for position. And the end result is that often the most talented guy doesn't win. But the *better* guy does. Because being a distance runner isn't just about stamina and speed. It's about guts and heart, instinct and mental toughness. It's also about brains.

And that was Matthew's great edge, I thought, heading into this race. He's smart, he's aggressive, and he's tough. I knew he had worked through his strategies a thousand times and was ready to handle every conceivable way the race could unfold—fast or slow. Forty years ago, I stood on the line for the same race at the Montreal games. Like father, like son – I guess, but Mathew came with talent and preparation and confidence that I never had.

The 1500m has been kryptonite to Americans for over a century. The last time a U.S. runner won was Mel Shappard in 1908, the same year that the hard luck Chicago Cubs won their last World Series. Since then a host of different nationalities had taken gold, but in recent decades the event was dominated by North and East Africans. Algerians, Moroccans, and especially the Kenyans had dominated the Olympic middle and distance events and owned the world record books.

The consensus favorite in Rio was Asbel Kiprop, an otherworldly talent who won gold in Beijing in 2008 at only 19 years old, and who had won the last three world championships in a row. Only a hamstring injury kept him from repeating his victory at the 2012 London Olympic Games. He was back and healthy in Rio, and still very much in his prime at 27. And apart from that race at the 2012 Olympics where Kiprop injured his hamstring, Matthew had never beaten him.

Kiprop's personal record was 3:26.69, just a fraction of a second off the world record. Matthew, by comparison, had never run better than 3:30. Kiprop was a brilliant talent but he could be erratic, and always seemed to avoid taking an early lead in a race, even when it was to his advantage. In Rio, Kiprop had showboated his way through the qualifying heats, running each one in dead last place and then shooting to the front seemingly on a whim. But this time, I knew Matthew was ready for him. Matthew and his coach, Alberto Salazar, had already prepared precisely for just that kind of move.

Matthew had a confidence building within him that I'd rarely seen in any runner, much less my own son. His final workouts
4

under Alberto were extraordinary. He had run a 1:47 in an 800m race in Oregon just two weeks earlier, and Alberto had Matthew follow up that same day with three more 800's immediately after at 1:53, 1:49, and 1:47. At practice in Rio he'd been running 400s, with his fastest as low as 49—the kind of leg speed I never had on my fastest day. I was confident the morning of that race that no matter the outcome Matthew was ready to throw down and be a real factor in the race.

Sitting there in the stands, waiting for the start, I couldn't help but think of two final factors that gave me confidence. First, the officials added a 13th runner to a normally 12-man race, because of a disqualification in the semis that had negatively affected two runners. This meant if Kiprop continued his tactic of running in the back and saving strength for the final 600m he'd have even more traffic to fight through.

Second, the start of the finals was delayed for nearly twenty minutes because NBC was holding on the gold medal soccer match between Brazil and Germany that had gone late into penalty kicks. With so long between warmup and the race, I knew that the more anxious athletes would be shaken by the delay. The more experienced runners would have a huge advantage. I knew Mathew wouldn't be rattled, knew he would stay calm, that's his temperament. Then, just as the finalists were brought to the starting line for introductions, I saw Matthew on the stadium's big screen. There he was. My boy.

One of the more amazing things about being someone in my shoes—an ex-runner, a seasoned track coach, and a guy who has watched his kid follow in his footsteps—is that you've seen them run so many times that you know how they're going to compete just by watching them warm up, do their strides and stand on the starting line. I don't know how it works or what it is, whether it's just reading his body language, seeing a facial expression, or some more complicated sixth sense, but I know it when I see it. That night, I knew in my bones that Matthew was ready to run.

But, then again, like I said, until the race starts, nobody really knows anything.

As they toed the line, while the announcer ran through the names of the contestants, I could tell right away from Kiprop's body language that he was prepared to cede the lead, just as he had done in the heats and in the semi. And despite his extensive experience, he also looked a bit uneasy with the delay.

The gun fired, and immediately Kiprop gave a leisurely first dozen strides, clearly avoiding the pack jockeying for the front. Matthew on the other hand was fourth from the rail and shot forward. It was unusual for him to grab an early lead, but nobody else seemed willing to take it so Matthew assumed command. Kiprop, as expected, drifted into last place, his long loping strides making him look like a man out for a morning jog.

Matthew almost seemed to be daring the pack behind him to run as slow as possible. He led the first lap to a glacial pace of 66 seconds. The second was even slower: 69.7. The race was unbelievably slow, as slow as a high school dual meet. Something was going to happen soon, but who would move first and when would they go? Had Alberto run through this exact scenario with Matthew? As prepared as they were, it seemed unlikely that they could have foreseen Matthew leading the pack through 800 meters at 2:16.

In the middle of the second lap, though, well behind Matthew, Kiprop finally got fed up being behind the whole pack at such a slow pace and burst forward on the backstretch. The sudden move caused those keying off Kiprop to react. Moving wide to follow, Algeria's Souleimon clipped the heel of Kemoi–the second Kenyan in the field—sending Kemoi sprawling to the ground and forcing two other runners to vault over the fallen man.

Kiprop seemed unfazed by the fracas and was now just a few strides behind Matthew and the other leaders, and by the beginning of the third lap he was once again perfectly poised to make one of his signature moves. My palms were sweating, my mouth was dry, I was more nervous than I'd ever been. With 700m to go, my son was leading in the Olympic finals with the world's fastest milers all just inches behind him.

The next 100 seconds would be the most exciting of Matthew's life, and—by extension—my own.

CHAPTER TWO: THE BRONX

Track saves people. I believe that. As a runner, a coach, and a father, I've seen it time and time again.

At the very least, it saved me.

In the summer of 1969 it felt like the world was falling apart. I'd say I finished eighth grade, but survived is more accurate. I flunked every class—every single class—and missed school over 50% of the time. My school, PS 22, was one of the worst in the Bronx, with one of the city's highest truancy rates—and I was its best truant.

But it wasn't just me. For generations, the Bronx was a rock-solid, working-class neighborhood that had its share of wise guys, but it was mostly full of working families, where mothers stayed home and fathers went to work in the nearby factories. But in 1969 it had started to spin apart. The families that were doing well got out, leaving only the families, like mine, that were struggling.

I don't know what the reason was, or even if there was just one reason. Some say it was the newly built Cross Bronx Expressway that sliced old neighborhoods in half and turned the blocks on either side into slums. Some that it was the growth of the suburbs luring the higher income people out, and discriminatory redlining policies kept people of color from following. Others say it was the death of the Tammany machine that, despite the corruption and graft, kept the city running smoothly. The factories that the Bronx was once famous for were closing left and right, and that didn't help either.

In any case, all I know is almost overnight the neighborhood got much poorer. And the Irish, Jewish, Polish, Italian, and German faces in the streets outside my flat suddenly became Puerto Rican ones. Even the president of the whole Borough of the Bronx—once the same Italian guy for almost 30 years— was now a Puerto Rican. As a kid, of course, I didn't have any problem with all the new neighbors. They talked different, cooked different food, played different music. The neighborhood was full of unfamiliar smells and sounds. But they didn't make the place poorer, they just came in because the rent was cheap.

White flight made the property values drop like crazy, so landlords started burning their own buildings to collect on the insurance. Sometimes tenants got a tip-off, sometimes they didn't. The arson got so bad they eventually had to change the insurance laws. All the while the city was closing fire stations due to budget cuts. By the mid-70s parts of the south Bronx looked like a war zone—buildings turned to rubble and nothing built in their place. And despite all that, it was still my neighborhood, it was home, and I had to try to make it work for me.

The first day of junior high I wore a white shirt and tie, like I always did in elementary school, and I went in the boys' bathroom. It was like a nightclub. Kids were smoking in there and drinking wine—early in the morning before class. I took that tie off real quick and learned how to dress a lot different, and started transforming into a screw-up just like everybody else.

So the only learning I did in those years was in the streets with my friends. We drank, we smoked cigarettes, we smoked pot. I was in every kind of trouble there was. I was trying to be a big shot. We weren't serious criminals by any means, but we were going nowhere fast. I was on my way to being a low-level hoodlum, but plenty of guys around me were already hardened criminals.

One Thanksgiving weekend I was locked up in juvenile hall because they found marijuana in my locker. There was a whole different kind of human being in there. I saw really bad fights. I saw a guy get raped. It was terrifying stuff for a 13-year-old to witness. I realized then that I never wanted to go back. They labeled me a PINS: A Person in Need of Supervision, which is what I was. Not a fundamentally bad kid, just someone who wanted to grow up too fast, be a man before I knew what being a man even was.

And then to make it even worse: my parents split up. It was always a difficult marriage. My mother, Theresa Corrigan, was a first-generation immigrant, sailing to New York from Ireland at the age of 15 and working as a maid most of her life. My father, Sid Centrowitz, was Jewish, and grew up in the Bowery in Manhattan and became a professional gambler. In a way, he was impressive. He was the only Jewish gambler allowed to run a card house in Little Italy in the West Bronx. And by all accounts he ran it well. They didn't drink, didn't mess around with any nonsense, they just kept the action going. Sometimes they'd stay up for 24 hours easy, three or four days with minimal sleep, just to keep people gambling. He was entertaining, he was funny. And he was good at getting people to lose their money. He worked for the mob, of course, and he would get a cut. And he would skim some money off the top.

My father had a sick view on society. But it came with the era. Everyone had a vice – drinking, drugs, women – and my father chose to gamble. As with any addiction, there were massive highs and traumatic lows. He was extremely controlling. We had to eat exactly as much food as he put on the plate—no more, no less. When we rode in the car we all had permanent assigned seats. It was like the military.

One day, it became too much for my mother. Her doctor told her if she didn't leave, she'd have a nervous breakdown. So, when I was nine, she left. And because the law at the time disallowed children of different genders to sleep in the same bedroom, she could only afford to take my sister, Maureen and for three years we only saw our mother on weekends. The upside was that my mother, who was a nervous wreck when she was with my father, became almost a totally different person. She understood the stresses we were under and became more of a friend in a lot of ways. So, while I saw her less, she became a bigger part of my life.

For those three years my younger brother Gerald and I lived with my father—who only got worse after my mother left him—and waited for my mother to save enough money to afford a two-bedroom apartment. When that day finally came, my brother and I didn't hesitate. We chose our mother. Instead of taking this like a man, my father cut us off. He decided he wanted nothing to do with us. And the last thing he said to me was, "You'll never amount to anything without me."

That's about the worst you could ever say to a 12-year-old. I didn't see him at all for the next seven years.

***

By 1969, sensing that I was headed down a path as bad as my father's, my mother moved us out of the Bronx. She quit her job, went on welfare, and moved us out to Queens. Now Queens and the Bronx may look close on a map, especially if you're not from New York, but to me it was a whole different world. It took two-and-a-half hours to get there using public transportation. For better or worse, I was leaving my old life entirely behind.

It may sound like there was nothing to miss about the Bronx, but that's not exactly true. One great thing, maybe the best thing, about my old neighborhood is that we lived just two blocks away from Yankee Stadium. And in the 50s and 60s the Yankees were the absolute pinnacle of the sports world for the whole country. They were the best, most glamorous team in a sport that was then America's undisputed pastime. And I got into games for free.

My older sister was a looker—or so they said—and to earn points with her the older boys in the neighborhood who worked the games would let us in for free (saving us the quarter a ticket would cost). We'd bring our own lunch and have to sit in the bleachers, but as the game wore on and the suit-and-tie crowd from Manhattan and the suburbs left early, we'd sneak down to the good seats. Nobody ever minded. It was kid-friendly in those days.

And I didn't just love baseball, I loved what the Yankees represented. They were winners. Even in the rare years they weren't winning the World Series (they won 8 between 1950 and 1962 alone) they were still 'Winners.' Mickey Mantle and Roger Maris weren't just great players; they were like aristocrats. The crowd wore white shirts and ties, the food was better, the stadium was better. It was a whole organization built on a self-reinforcing culture of winning.

My mother also loved baseball—she went to Yankee games often and always religiously kept score on her score card. She even taught my brother and I to throw and catch. Even when he was still around, my father worked seven days a week, so we barely saw him—but my mom taught us a lot about baseball when we were younger. She was very athletic for a woman in those days—completely unlike my father who was fat and slow. Tall, always thin, with unusually big feet, she played street games with her brothers, and with us kids—and sometimes I wonder what kind of success she could have had if she had been born in a different era.

There was no Little League at that time in the Bronx. We'd either play stick ball or curb ball. Curb ball had all the rules of baseball but no batter or pitcher. Instead you had a Thrower who throw the ball at the corner point on the curb and the ball would bounce back into the "field of play." Fly ball could be caught out, ground ball you'd have to throw out. You run around the bases same as baseball. Depending on time of day it could get kind of hairy. Cars coming by. Sometimes they'd interfere--that was just bad luck. Sometimes a kid got hit by a car.

We played other games: touch football and sometimes sewer-to-sewer races. We raced by height, so because I was taller than average I was usually racing older kids. It didn't mean that much to me then, but I won more than I lost.

The thing I later tried to drill into my own kids is that back then we organized ourselves. There was no higher authority to appeal to—you had to negotiate. The older kid told you the ball was out, you had two choices: you either hit him and get beat up, or you take your lumps and you look like a schmoe.

A bunch of guys who didn't mind looking like schmoes were the New York Mets. Their first two years, in 1962 and 1963, the Mets played in the old Polo Grounds that the New York Giants abandoned when they relocated to the West Coast along with the rival Dodgers. The corny Mets not only used another team's stadium scraps, they took their colors too—combining the Giants' orange with Dodger blue into a color combination that made them look like clowns. Even their own manager—former Yankee great Casey Stengel—seemed to think the whole thing was a joke. He cracked wise about his terrible players to the press, who ate it up.

The Polo Grounds were in upper Manhattan, a short walk from our apartment in the Bronx. But I rarely went. Not only was the product on the field a wreck, but the losing attitude extended to the crowd. No ties, that's for sure. Most of the time they were drunk, falling down, fighting, you name it. They even drank a different beer—Rheingold instead of Yankee Stadium's classier Shaefer Beer.

Pretty early on I could tell the difference between a winning environment and a losing one.

And guess where those Mets had moved in 1964? You got it: Queens. And here I was following in their footsteps. The crazy thing was, the year I moved, 1969, the "Miracle Mets" shocked the world—their own fans most of all—by winning the World Series. But that was in October, and when school started after Labor Day all I knew was that I wasn't in the Bronx anymore. While the Bronx had what felt like a whole new population overnight, Queens had the same traditional mix of working

17

class whites and blacks, but still, change was coming from within.

Our part of Queens was almost entirely black and for the first time I saw signs of what had been going on throughout the country in the 60s. People were outside protesting in the street. Vietnam. Black power. There wasn't anything resembling conformity. Anything that could be rebelled against, was. My mother enrolled me in Andrew Jackson High School, a school that had police officers stationed within the school. The school had proud traditions, but was caught up in the chaos of the times—in fact just a few years after I left, the police actually shut down a heroin factory that was operating in the basement of the school.

Kids weren't just cutting classes here; they were in open revolt. Flipping a teacher's car over outside. They'd be sucker punching people, even the teachers. I saw a teacher get beat up by students—that opened my eyes.

So, I don't know what would have happened to me if I hadn't had the sense to listen up in gym class that first day.

"Track tryouts. Today. 3pm. See Coach Blatt out by the track."

I thought, okay, this is something. Maybe I can do this.

I already knew I was fast. And that I liked running. We played games more than raced, but the older I got the more I won those sewer-to-sewer races. But for most of my life I had no idea competitive running even existed. A baseball player runs down the base path, a football player runs down the field, but a whole sport just dedicated to running? It was news to me. But the 1968 Mexico City Olympics changed all that.

Track and field may have been unknown to young kids in the Bronx but on the world stage, in the Olympics, it was the centerpiece. The best athletes on earth competed for national pride at the height of the Cold War. The Yankees may have won the World Series, but it's not like the Russians cared. Every country on earth wanted to win the 400m.

On my black and white TV I watched, riveted, event after event. 200m, 400m, 800m, 4x400m, 1500m, hurdles, steeplechase, marathon—I had no idea so many running events existed. It seemed like every country in the world was competing for these medals and the Americans were winning a bunch of them. In the 400, Americans cleaned up, taking home gold, silver, and bronze, with my new hero Lee Evans decimating the world record in 43.86 (which to this day still has him in the top ten fastest quarter-milers of all time). I consumed every minute of Olympic track and field, especially the events that the Americans were winning. You see, unlike today where we have hundreds of channels to watch on television, or websites to visit on the internet, back in 1968, we only had one of three networks to watch. So, when something like the Olympics came on, everybody watched, especially kids like me looking for role models. During those games, track athletes like Bob Beamon, Jim Hines, Bill Toomey, Lee Evans and Tommie Smith all became household names. And Evans and Smith, because of their bold Black Power salute, became even bigger than that—they were icons (and, to some, villains).

I honestly didn't understand the politics at the time, but when Evans anchored a 4x400 relay team that also blew away the world record—and the nearest competition by almost 50 meters – I was hooked. Running the lead leg on that blazingly fast relay team was young guy named Vince Matthews. And where did Matthews—who would later win an individual 400m gold of his own in Munich 1972—come from? You guessed it: Andrew Jackson High School in Queens, New York.

So, you could say the tryouts got my attention.

I learned that not only did Andrew Jackson produce Matthews, Coach Blatt had trained Julio Meade, who was then an All-American sprinter at Kansas, and Andrew Jackson had the standing national high school record for the 4x880, a record— 7:35.6, set in 1966—that would stand for almost 25 years. Olympians? All-Americans? National records? I knew then that this Coach Blatt had to be a hell of a coach. I thought I was pretty fast—at least I could beat anyone my age in the sewer-to-sewer races in the Bronx—so maybe this coach could make something out of me? I sure didn't have anything to lose by trying.

I showed up that afternoon in my beat-up sneakers and cotton shorts and shirt that still smelled of sweat from gym class, ready to prove myself.

"Freshmen! Line up over here," Blatt yelled. I drifted over to a corner of the track with maybe two or three dozen other kids. As with the larger student body, I was one of the only white kids.

"No, kid, what are you doing?" I heard, as I was shuffling through the crowd. Somebody must have been goofing off. I looked around to see what the offender had been caught doing. Instead I saw the legendary Coach Milt Blatt staring dead at me.

"You," he said, "You kidding me? You're no freshman."

At that point I was a big kid, at least for those days. 5'10", 175 lbs. Most of it muscle. Compared to the skinny freshmen around me, I looked like a football player.

Sheepishly I protested, "I am, sir."

"How old are you?"

"Fourteen."

He shook his head. Clearly he didn't believe me, but wasn't going to waste any more time on some white kid who probably wouldn't make the team. "If you're still here tomorrow, bring a birth certificate."

I nodded, hoping my mother hadn't left my certificate back in the Bronx.

"Okay, first eight of you, line up. Take a lane. No horsing around.," he said, walking back over to the finish line. "Hundred-yard dash. End of the straightaway here. Full sprint, okay? Run like men."

A little humiliated at being called out on my size, I hung back and watched the first group go off at his starter's pistol. He had his own stop watch and a clipboard, conferring with each of the kids at the end of each heat to get their names.

The sewer to sewer races we ran were about 25 or 30 yards. Sometimes we'd run two sewers at 50 or 60. Any more than that was basically guaranteeing a car or something would interfere and spoil the race. But this 100 on a flat straightaway seemed manageable. At least I wouldn't have to keep an eye out of the corner of my eye for a cement truck.

Finally, at the third or fourth heat I lined up in the far outside lane, a stocky white kid next to all these lanky black and Dominican guys, and dug the bald rubber heel of my worn-out sneaker into the cinder track.

Crack! The starting pistol went off and I churned my legs. Did I think at that time I was bound for greatness? Not really. I just wanted to make the team. Just to have some kind of purpose. To be good at something, anything. And maybe to have somebody like Coach Blatt respect me.

Whatever that was—hunger, desperation, hope—it pushed me. I crossed the finish line a full stride ahead of all the other kids. Not even panting I jogged over to Coach Blatt.

"Name?"

"What was my time?" I asked, not even knowing then what a good time was.

He ignored my question. "Name?"

"Centrowitz, Matthew."

Blatt didn't even look up, writing my name in pencil on his clipboard.

"Okay, Centrowitz. Bring your birth certificate tomorrow." And with that he turned to the next kid, "Name?"

So, I was on the team.

CHAPTER THREE: ANDREW JACKSON

I knew so little about running that it was news to me that in the fall we'd be running cross country instead of track and field events. Having been only familiar with running through the Olympics I was a little disappointed. My dream of being the next Lee Evans would have to wait a few months, but I quickly embraced it, figuring I was so new I'd have time to get in shape before the "real" season started.

Cross-country in the middle of a metropolis like New York City was kind of a funny concept. There wasn't a whole lot of country. In fact, at that point I'd never once left the city in my entire life, so "country" to me was everything else outside of New York. Rural, cows, fishing. In short: boring. New York didn't have any fields and cows, but we did have city parks, and at Andrew Jackson we mostly ran at nearby Cunningham Park.

In those days in New York we ran 2.5 mile routes for cross country. The first day of practice after school, Coach Blatt lead us not out to the track but to a city bus, and we rode a few stops over to Cunningham Park, which had a cross country course. Now I had never in my life run so much as a quarter mile at once without stopping, much less more than two, but it's not like I knew where my limit was either. I was never doubled over after running out an "inside the park" home run in stickball. Or taking an interception back the other way in touch football. I ran that 100-yard tryout so easily, maybe this would be easy too. Wrong.

I couldn't believe how bad I did, and even more, how bad I felt. I thought I was a big strong kid, fast and in great shape. And I was dying. Sucking wind, nauseous. Legs felt a million pounds. Worse than the physical feeling was the humiliation. I was way at the back of the pack. Even the sprinters who acted like cross country was something of a joke beat me. To add insult to injury, half the guys who finished ahead of me that day whipped out cigarettes and started smoking on the walk back to the bus. How sad is that?

On the bus ride back, I felt like quitting. I felt awful, my shoes, shirt and shorts looked like shit. I didn't need to do this and I hated being humiliated, but something inside told me that even though I may have underestimated how much 2 ½ miles would kick my ass, I had a lot more to prove. So, the next day I hit it again with even more determination and knocked a full minute off my time. By the third day, I was in the middle of the pack. At least I wasn't getting embarrassed anymore.

Soon I was one of the better distance guys on the team. Coach Blatt, never one to offer much in the way of praise—or excess words of any kind—one day walked up to me and said, "You're a miler." He said so, and that was it. That was my identity now.

Almost overnight I fell in love with running. A lot of the sprinters hated the grind of the cross country season but I loved it. I'd have run even further if coach let me, but he never did. I wanted to be fast, and I wanted to be respected. I especially loved the idea of getting better. That's what drove me, getting better and better with every run. As soon as I stepped into this world, I knew there was no way I was going back to the old one.

I loved to train, and loved being part of the team. The older guys couldn't have been more encouraging. Here I was this half-Jewish, half-Irish stocky white freshman on a nearly all-black team. But they were tremendously supportive. A few of the seniors in particular took me under their wing, said I could be really good. I'd never had an older kid mentor me like that, look out for me. It seems like a small thing but it meant the world to me.

27

There was one big problem though: I couldn't race. Money was always tight at home, even more so now that my mother was on welfare. So, Fridays and Saturdays I had to go back to the Bronx and make money delivering meat for a butcher who was a friend of the family. The big meets were always on Saturday, so I'd train all week but never had the opportunity to prove myself.

To Coach Blatt's credit he didn't give me any grief for doing it. Some coaches would have kicked me off their team if I wasn't able to race. Blatt was one of the best coaches in the city—his athletes had won some of the most storied races in New York history. But he had been teaching and coaching a long time. He was at Andrew Jackson the year in opened in 1937 (originally he coached tennis—his personal sport, and only got into track because nobody else would do it), and he saw how the neighborhood was changing. He knew I had no choice but to work that delivery job.

One day at school we had a half-day of classes with two hours to kill before practice started. Coach Blatt called me into his office and tells me he has a project for me, and he'll pay for my time. Always needing extra money, I say, sure. He wanted me to chronologically order a bunch of newspaper clippings he'd thrown in a manila folder. So, I sat there for two hours and read all these articles over the years about Andrew Jackson runners winning this race or that one, the incredible history of all the runners who came before me, who once—it occurred to me—were just wide-eyed freshmen like I was.

Blatt acted like it was just a nagging chore he needed help with, but he knew what he was doing. He was a master of psychology. He was spoon feeding me, and I was gobbling it up. Soon I was absolutely dying for the chance to race. Something I didn't realize at the time, but know now, is that the best coaches are really like psychologists – they can read your body and see what is going on in your head. More importantly, they know the keys to getting each athlete to unlock their potential – how to motivate, when to hold a kid back, when to push them harder. Blatt was like that.

I was dying to race, but for now, it simply wasn't an option. Bills still had to be paid, so I schlepped two-and-a-half hours back to the Bronx on Friday afternoon, slept at the butcher's house, and delivered meat all day on Saturday while my friends on the team competed back over in Queens.

I'd take deliveries from the butcher shop to apartments all over the neighborhood. Most of the orders were for older people living on higher floors in buildings with no elevator. Not a coincidence—they didn't want to walk their own groceries up, so better to pay some crazy kid like me to do it. I would carry as much as I could so it would shorten the routes. I'd go

29

out, with maybe 40 or 50 pounds of meat—close to Thanksgiving I'd have three, sometimes four whole turkeys—in shopping bags, up staircase after staircase and then run back.

I even made a game of it, timing myself on runs back after killing my legs on the stairs. It was harder than any track practice, I can tell you that. I was cross training before anybody knew what cross-training was. Years later, when the movie *Rocky* came out, and I saw Stallone punching slabs of beef to prepare for his big fight, I couldn't help but laugh at the similarity. "Try carrying 'em up six flights in January," I wanted to yell at the screen.

By the end of the season, Coach Blatt in his quiet, subtle way had me worked into a frenzy to compete. So, the final Saturday I begged off work in order to compete in my very first cross country race: The Public School Athletic League championships (PSALs). Over 20 schools from all five boroughs would be there. Well over 100 runners.

This race was in Van Cortland Park, a massive recreation area and green space (even bigger than Central Park) on the northern edge of city. I had no idea at the time, but Van Cortland is something of a national mecca for cross country running—first laid out in 1913. The terrain was much different than anything I'd ever seen before. The trail twisted and turned, the woods around were dense and dark, and the trail itself broken up by roots and rocks.

And then there was the hill the upper-classmen were telling me about on the ride over. "Don't hit the wall before you get to that hill." Cemetery Hill, so named, because the original Van Cortland's had a family burial plot there. But to us it was a punishing slope on the backside of the course where weak runners went to die.

For the first time I found myself with runners outside of my own team. I had never seen any of them before, and I realized—as they were gawking at me—none of them had seen me all season either. It was the Freshman Championship race, and here I was, bigger than all of them and coming out of nowhere just in time for the last race of the year. But at this point, I think I was just a novelty. My body type was so different from those other runners I don't think they considered me a serious threat.

But I was.

Coach Blatt told me flat out I could win. In retrospect, it seems crazy: my very first race, beating every freshman in the city. But if he said it, I believed it. The strategy was simple. Stay close to the lead guy, no more than a stride or two behind, and then in the last quarter mile, kick into a sprint and win. That was it. "When you can see the finish line, go win," was about all he said. Made sense to me. So, I did it.

Maybe it was all those stairs with the meat deliveries. Maybe I was just a little fresher than everybody else from not competing all season. Maybe I just too naïve to know how hard that course was. Or, hey, maybe I was just that good. But I won. There were more than a couple of hundred kids in that race and I won. It felt amazing. And I knew that I needed that feeling again.

My teammates were ecstatic. All the upper classmen crowded around to congratulate me. And it may have been a trick of the light, but even Coach Blatt looked like he smiled there for a second.

But the coaches and runners from the other teams weren't exactly humble in defeat.

"Who is this guy? He's a ringer."

"This kid can't be fricking 14. He's got to be at least 17."

"He must be using his younger brother's birth certificate."

It may seem funny in retrospect, but it really hurt. Hearing this from the coaches, whose respect I wanted more than anything, was brutal. Even the ones who didn't question my age predicted I was a flash in the pan, that I would never get any better because I was too big. For the first time in my life I was doing everything the right way, playing by the rules, not cutting corners, and they assumed I was cheating. I came away from that day with not just the exhilarating feeling of triumph but this sting of embarrassment, that despite winning I somehow still didn't belong.

And it was a world to which I badly wanted to belong. Cross country season ended and indoor track began. I still had to work the meat delivery job Fridays and Saturdays and wouldn't be able to race, but running became my life. It became the reason behind everything else I did.

Indoor season meant speed work, a 180 from the cross country practices. Coach Blatt's training was all about hard, short intervals. You would go all out—bang! And then you would rest. All out—bang! Then rest. Half the workouts I would finish and ask Coach "I'm not that tired, can I do more?" I never remembering him saying yes.

In retrospect, it's a big reason why Andrew Jackson produced great sprinters and middle distance runners, but no top tier long distance guys. I was something of an anomaly. But even though Blatt may not have maximized my training regimen that year, he was doing something far more important: he was helping to raise me. He was making me a man.

I was kind of amazed how much Coach Blatt believed in me. One day he told me that I could go to college. This stunned me. Nobody in my family went to college. Not a single person I knew growing up in the south Bronx had been to college, except teachers. But he said it—and if he said it, he meant it.

Overnight I went from the goof off who barely attended 50% of his classes to a kid who never once missed a class and was maintaining a 90 average. Because I was on a team, I got out of gym class, and Coach Blatt arranged to have me tutored by one of his best runners, Phil Kreitzer. He ran the anchor on the 4x880, the relay that made Andrew Jackson nationally famous and a team I badly wanted to get on.

Coach thought that not only could I use the academic help; I'd benefit from the mentorship of runner I respected. He was right.

As I reflect now, I wonder how much I also benefited from the turbulence of those times. In a less chaotic environment, even though I was working as hard as I could, I'm not sure I would have cut the mustard in class. But it was 1969—kids were bailing on school, rebelling against everything. Some of my classrooms were almost empty. So simply by showing up, sitting up front and working hard, I found myself getting A's. Honestly I wasn't that smart, and I was playing catch up from years of not learning a thing. In reality I was no A student. But

I sat up front, did all my homework, and showed Coach Blatt every A I received. It's funny how one person looking out for them can help a kid turn his life around.

My personal life too became totally dedicated to success out on the track. I would sit through what felt like endless bowling or some other pointless game on ABC's *Wide World of Sports* to get to the track and field events at the end. I went to bed every night at 10pm. Coach told me that athletes should get nine hours of sleep, so I got my nine hours religiously. I didn't smoke cigarettes anymore, didn't smoke pot, never drank. I didn't even have a girlfriend. Years later I'd cringe at how often I turned down opportunities from girls in the neighborhood. I had seen this Burt Lancaster movie on TV about Jim Thorpe, and he lived like a monk—just trained and studied and won races. I thought that's how you had to do it, like Jim Thorpe. I didn't associate with anybody from the old neighborhood.

A whole new world had opened up for me, and as soon as I stepped into that world I knew there was no way I was ever going back.

***

By spring I had saved up enough money from those freezing days of work, trudging up slippery staircases and running back through the snow, to finally quit the delivery job and compete on Saturdays. Coach never pressured me, but I could tell he was pleased. He put me on the 4x880 relay. As a freshman I got the third leg—typically for the slowest guy, even though I was the second fastest—but all that mattered was I was out there, winning races, competing with other schools, starting to make a name for myself as a Track Man.

At that time in New York City, we weren't called runners, we were called "Track Men." We warmed up, we warmed down, we never stepped off the track. Once you stepped off the track, you were done, practice was over. Track Men stayed on the track.

There was no such thing as road running in those days. They say it was born in the 1960s, but honestly that was just a bunch of crazy guys running around the city, older guys running away from their demons. To us they weren't really athletes, they were eccentrics. New York City wouldn't even hold its first marathon—with a grand total of 55 runners, all men—until 1970, and it was entirely in Central Park, not on the city streets.

Unlike the cross country races held way out in the parks, the spring track and field meets were well attended. For our school, at least, it was the big spring sport. There was no soccer, no women's sports of any kind yet, and our baseball team stunk. And track was an Olympic sport, people respected it. So, the bleachers at these meets were pretty full—it was about as good a free entertainment as a high schooler was going to find on a Saturday.

All season long I ran that third leg of the relay, and was thrilled to do it, but a growing part of me wanted to prove that I was in fact the miler that Coach Blatt said I was. And I couldn't exactly do that until I actually ran the mile.

Blatt was insistent that nobody at those distances run a double. So, if I ran the 4x880, that was it, that was my race for the day. I told him I had plenty of time to recover, that I wasn't fatigued. But he didn't budge.

Finally, yet again, for the last race of the year, the PSALs, he let me compete in the 9th grade mile race. I didn't have a single mile time on record so I'm not sure how he qualified me for it—quite possibly just on his personal reputation. All he said to me before the race was, "Freshman state record is 4:28."

And in straightforward fashion I did it again. Led the whole way, pulled away at the end. Won by a good two three seconds. But there was less grumbling this time, less muttering that it was some kind of fluke. People were starting to realize I wasn't going away anytime soon. At 4:30 I narrowly missed the state freshman record, and for the first time I raised eyebrows. I even got offered free sneakers from Puma, which my coach made me turn down. And with that time, I was now on the national scene.

Now of course in those days there was no internet. News and times from races on the other side of the city, much less the other side of the country, took some time. Like every other coach in the country, Blatt subscribed to *Track & Field News*, the bible of competitive running which was published monthly with notable times and races around the country. Even more important, though, was the word of mouth that we track men shared with one another at meets.

"You should have seen this guy run the 880."

"This kid fell down in the first 100 of the mile, got up, and slowly pulled everybody in and won. It was incredible."

"His stride is something else, so fluid. You've gotta see it."

Unless it was truly exceptional, a fast time on paper could mean a lot of things. Wind, temperature, altitude, track conditions all varied. But another runner vouching for a guy, that meant the most. And now, finally, both my time and my performance were getting talked about.

As usual Coach Blatt said the least of all, but also the most. "You can break four minutes."

***

The four-minute mile was one of those magic numbers in sports. Even people who don't follow running know it. Batting .400. Rushing for 2,000 yards. Bowling a perfect game. It was the mark of somebody not merely good, but elite. Doctors once claimed the four-minute mile was physically impossible to break, and it had only finally been conquered in 1954 by Roger Bannister. 1954 seems like ancient history today but then it was just 16 years earlier, basically the short length of my own lifetime.

Fewer than 40 Americans ever had broken four-minutes at that point, and just three high schoolers: Jim Ryun, Tim Danielson, and Marty Liquori. Jim Ryun was the first, hitting 3:59 as a junior and then breaking his own record with a 3:55.3 his senior year in 1965—a U.S. high school record that would stand until 2001. (At that time Jim Ryun held the world record in the mile at 3:51.1 and was coincidentally out at Kansas

University running with recent Andrew Jackson graduate Julio Meade.)

The freshman record—which I had just the one chance to break—was 4:28. But the larger New York state high school record was 4:06. If Blatt thought I could break four minutes, I'd be entering the realm of not just impressive, not just promising, but truly top talent in the country.

So even more than my wins and my time, Coach Blatt's simple faith made me believe I was capable of something much greater.

I didn't have any idea then, but a *Sports Illustrated* cover that June was a harbinger of my own future. For the first time I could remember, *Sports Illustrated*, the undisputed sports magazine of the era, had on its cover not just a runner but a distance runner. Mid-stride, with his jaw jutted out, half open, running up some kind of mountain, surrounded by more trees than I'd ever seen in my life, was this handsome young kid. He wore dark green shorts and a light green undershirt underneath a yellow jersey with "OREGON" printed in bold green letters. Oregon? Way out there with the lumberjacks and the beavers? The cover read "America's Distance Prodigy – Freshman Steve Prefontaine."

Of course he was a freshman in college, not high school like me, but the fact that he captured the cover of America's premiere sports publication just as a freshman was striking. At that point I was happy just to get a time listed in the newspaper or *Track & Field News*. This guy's picture was on the coffee table of half the homes in the country.

I tore into the article eager to see what kind of feats had earned him this fame. The star of the piece was Prefontaine of course, but it also heavily featured his coach at the University of Oregon, Bill Bowerman. Bowerman sounded like General McArthur: tough, stingy with praise, dry sense of humor. And, surprising to me, he insisted his athletes call him Bill and not "coach." Making a cameo in the piece was a man who would go on to play a huge role in my life, Bowerman's "young and very capable assistant" Bill Dellinger, though I can't say his name even registered at the time.

Overall it was a puff piece, making Prefontaine out to be the next great American runner, though he clearly had a long way to go to take the crown from guys like Ryun and Liquori. And his times were very good—particularly his three-mile time at 13:12—his tactics relentless, his attitude mature. But one thing stood out to me more than anything else: his high school freshman mile time.

I'd just run a 4:30 in my first-ever mile and this celebrated runner, America's running hero, had, as a high school freshman, run a 5:00 mile.

Here I come, Pre.

CHAPTER FOUR: POWER MEMORIAL

That spring, I quit my job at the butchers and my mother took one as a personal maid in Queens. In one of those lucky breaks—call it fate, call it whatever you want—the woman's son was an administrator at Power Memorial High School in Manhattan. Power Memorial had an athletic tradition even greater than Andrew Jackson's, producing basketball greats like Kareem Abdul-Jabbar, Lenny Elmore, Mario Elie. And—it was not lost on me—it had just graduated the reigning state record holder in the mile, Tony Colon.

So, at the end of the school year, my mother decided I had turned things around enough to come back to the Bronx and try to get into this private school. At the time if you transferred public schools you lost two whole years of athletic eligibility. But because Power was a Catholic school, I could transfer over the summer and be immediately eligible. Her friend's son talked to the track coach, Brother Bielen, and the friar sent me a letter that read, "Our boy Tony Colon just ran 4:06 this past summer, and with your freshman times being ahead of him, I'm sure we can make you a sub-4 man by your senior year. However, there are a few matters we need to discuss. Please come in for an interview."

Power Memorial was an unusual building—a condemned children's hospital that stood ten stories high. The classrooms were all former wards, something that all the desks and chalkboards could never quite make you forget. I rode up a groaning old elevator to the top floor and soon found myself sitting in front of the desk of Brother Bielen, who served as track coach, biology teacher, and guidance counselor. He alone would have final say over my admission.

Brother Bielen had started his career at Leo High School in Chicago in 1962 and had coached the winning cross country teams in Chicago in 1966 and 1967. He had coached the USA Junior Olympic team. He brought a coaching system and philosophy to New York City that was very different from the standard at the time. Rigorously intelligent and methodical, Bielen had two master's degrees in psychology and biology, and during my high school career would finish his PhD in counseling and psychology at Fordham University. With what felt like total control over my future, he was deeply intimidating.

On Bielen's desk were two folders. One held my junior high records: my disastrous 7th and 8th grades, where I failed to pass a single class—in many not even coming close—and a truancy rate of over 50%. That folder contained not a single positive word about me.

The other folder was my lone year at Andrew Jackson. Perfect attendance. Passed the daunting Regents Exam that New York City required of all its students. 90% average. Nothing but positive comments from my teachers.

Brother Bielen looks down through his reading classes at one open folder, then the other, then back again, milking every last drop of tension out of the moment. I was beyond nervous, palms dripping with sweat, leaning more and more forward in my chair like some kind of caged animal. I'm ready to scream now, because I want to get into this school so badly I can taste it. I'm dying.

Finally, he looks up, perfectly calm, and asks "I have just one question for you." He held up a folder in each hand. "Which one of these young men are you?"

I leaped out of my seat, pointing at my 9th grade folder. "That's me! That's me!" I almost shocked him I shouted so loud. If I could, I would have jumped into his lap.

He thinks for a moment, and then stands. I don't know what to think. He reaches his hand across the desk. In almost a daze I reach back and shake his hand. "Okay," he said, "Welcome to Power Memorial."

***

Going from the Bronx to Queens had been an adjustment, but Power Memorial was a whole different world. For one, I had to pay. Even though Power was the cheapest Catholic High School in the state, I was paying $500 in tuition every year—nearly all of it out of my pocket. My mother just didn't make enough money as a maid to help me cover the cost. I worked in a deli back in the Bronx during the summer (and every summer for the rest of high school) and continued throughout the school year on Wednesday nights. Even then, there were so many things my teammates could afford that were out of reach to me. Sometimes the Brothers found way to make exceptions, but knowing that I was so often a charity case was hard for me to handle sometimes.

And even though my mother was Irish, I was only Catholic in the loosest sense. I had never been baptized. I never went to Mass. I had my father's Jewish name (I never went to synagogue either). And I found myself in religion class light years behind everybody. I knew who Jesus was but that was about it. Honestly, I was totally ignorant of the most basic religious teachings. I hadn't even read the Bible. Needless to say, my first year at Power was a tough one. In addition to the change and burden of having to cover my tuition, I had to buy a new coat and tie and actually dress like an adult again.

The demographics of the school were carefully balanced by the brothers, with close to 30% Puerto Rican (and other Caribbean) students, 20% black, and 50% white. There was good diversity in every class that never fluctuated too much. The Puerto Rican and black kids were all, like me, from the city. But a lot of the white students were driven in from the suburbs by parents who worked in Manhattan. Interestingly, at Power I found I had much more in common with the black and Puerto Rican students, which just goes to show that when it comes to diversity and culture, there's lots more to it than just what ethnic group you belong to. In this case, the experience of being a poor city kid bound all of us closer together than we would have been at a public school – the contrast of our lives against those suburban kids reminded us of how much we had in common.

At Power, classes were far more difficult than at Andrew Jackson, but I was just as motivated to keep my grades up and stay eligible. I asked questions, I worked hard, I showed up on time. I was a good, but not great student. But it was all in service of a larger cause: running.

Brother John Bielen was a very different coach than Coach Blatt, and a different man. For one, he had dedicated his life to the Congregation of Christian Brothers, a Catholic order dedicated to education that at the time had over 600 schools in the U.S. He thought deeply about running, but also about the larger psychological experience of the young athlete. In a 1975 interview with *The Running Experience Magazine* he wrote:

> *The track man must have a happy experience. He must enjoy the team concepts, the thrill of competition, the time spent in track. My job as coach is not only to provide the technical information but to facilitate the enjoyment of participation. I am convinced that 50% of the high school runners could be exceptional but for various distractions that get in their way, or perhaps, a lack of desire.*

He went on to outline his directives for the young track man:

> 1. *Stay healthy physically with proper diet and sufficient rest.*

2. *Develop a positive attitude towards self and life, this comes through freedom from worry and problems.*

3. *Work hard at practice every day.*

4. *Have confidence in the coach, the program, and yourself.*

5. *Love to win and be an envious loser.*

So Bielen shaped me into a better distance runner. I ran much more volume—unlike Blatt, he let me do more when I was hungry to push myself further—and the interval work focused on strength and pace. But he was also shaping me into a man.

I wasn't merely looking for a father figure then, I was looking for a father. My dad had been gone three years without any trace—my mother kept our name listed as Centrowitz in the white pages every time we moved, but he just didn't even bother.

Bielen was enormously hard working, like all the coaches I connected with throughout my life, and very driven. One spring I contracted mono and was slow in recovering. Bielen thought I was ready to compete again and put me on the 1600m anchor leg of the Distance Medley Relay. I felt awful but the belief he showed in me inspired me to go all out, run as hard as I could to validate that belief. But sometimes your body can only do so much. I ran terribly. I got smoked by

49

everybody, and for the first time in my life collapsed to the ground after staggering across the finish line, lying on my back to catch my breath and hope the aching in my whole body would abate.

I didn't understand it at the time, but Bielen was embarrassed. Not just embarrassed we lost—including to some schools that Power *never* lost to—but embarrassed that he had so clearly made a mistake in running me. So, to my shock, he kicked me. Or at least nudged me, hard. "Get up!" he said, hoping that I was feigning somewhat from my own embarrassment. But I really was that sick. That moment has stayed with me because I knew how much he cared about me. I knew he was a master motivator; but I also knew that this time he was wrong. He ran me when I was still ill and for a moment, he didn't want to admit this to himself. I thought that if I ever coached someday, it was a lesson to remember

Having said that, Brother Bielen was also incredibly forgiving. We had kids on the track team who were struggling in their lives. A lot of the city kids made some mistakes, sometimes big mistakes. But he never gave up on them. He would also advocate—usually with success—that throwing them out would only make them worse. He didn't believe in throwing anybody out. He felt that every student was worth the extra effort, that all of us could be saved. He was a lot like Father

Flanagan of Boys Town. He embodied Father Flanagan's saying that, "There are no bad boys, only bad environment, bad training, bad example, bad thinking."

One kid on the track team was rough housing with his best friend and accidentally pushed him straight through a glass window, completely decapitating his friend. The police were preparing to bring charges of manslaughter against him. Brother Bielen led the other brothers in rallying against it, in defense of the young man. The young man would have to live with the tragic accident the rest of his life—what use was there in punishing him? Who would benefit? And, as was often the case, Bielen won out.

Over the three years at Power I spent hours in his office, sometimes—I'll admit—in tears, dealing with problems in my life and at home. And he was always nurturing, but strong. The kind of man I knew I wanted to be.

Bielen inspired me to want to become a guidance counselor myself someday. He loved to win races as much as anybody, but more than that he wanted to help us grow up into good men. Now that I'm a coach I am able to do that in my own small way.

***

My relationship with Bielen flourished and so did my running. With Bielen's training and the maturation of my body I methodically brought down my mile time, race after race, closer to that elusive 4-minute barrier. I ran 4:13 my junior year and then my senior hit 4:02.7, a New York state high school record that stands to this day. I also set state high school records in the 1500m (3:43.4) and the single time I ran the 5,000m (14:17). And I narrowly missed—by a second— matching Marty Liquori's course record at the 2.5 mile cross country course in Van Cortland Park. I was easily the best high school distance runner in the state of New York.

I had become what I always wanted to be: a star. To all the teachers and administrators, I was important. Before I was invisible—just one more annoying kid to deal with. And now I'm being taken by the hand, having applications filled out for me, guided through ever step. The amount of positive attention was tremendous, and I'm not afraid to admit I loved it.

The next level of validation was college. I was already getting recruited, but by then my standards were even higher: I wanted to run for an elite program. By now I knew all about the famed program at Oregon—that canvas of green behind

Prefontaine on the *Sports Illustrated* cover—but my first choice was Villanova.

I fell in love with Villanova watching them compete at the Penn Relays. Coach Jumbo Elliott was already considered to be one of the greatest track coaches of all time, with eight NCAA team titles and athletes winning 82 NCAA crowns. Jumbo Elliott was bigger than life. He was like God in the East coast track circuit. His teams dominated events from the quarter mile to the longer distances. Under Jumbo, Villanova produced five Olympic gold medal winners between 1956 and 1968. Everything about Villanova seemed great. Even their uniforms were the best. Oregon may have had Pre but Villanova had Marty Liquori, the phenom from New Jersey who had qualified for the Olympics at 19. Liquori was an instant TV star, boldly declared his intention to be the first millionaire distance runner, and was ranked number one in the world in the 1500m (he missed the 1972 Olympics due to injury).

Villanova recruited heavily from New York and New Jersey, and there was nobody in high school that year with more success on the track from the New York than me. So, in December of my senior year, as I expected, they came after me. Bielen was old school in demanding that all recruitment come through him. He said he wanted assurances that his athlete was going to be successful, and be important to the program. Frankly I think he just wanted his ass kissed. Either way he got it.

Coach Elliot told Bielen he was interested in offering me a scholarship and invited us down to Philadelphia on a recruiting trip. We took the Amtrak down there, and I met the team. Marty had graduated and was now training in Florida, but I met great runners like Kenny Schappert, Kevin McCarey, Eamonn Coghlan, and John Hartnett, who had just run a 3:54.7 mile. We got along great, and one of the guys who was a recent Power grad even invited me to be his roommate next year. It felt like a done deal. And then I was ushered into Jumbo's office to meet the famous coach.

I could tell in an instant it was over. His eyes said it all. He took one look at me and closed his mind. I was too big to be a good distance runner. How many times had I heard this before, "You're too big, kid, too big to be a middle distance runner". So, what if Liquori was my height (though nearly 20 pounds lighter than my muscular 170-lb frame). Right then, it didn't matter if I had any potential at all. All that mattered was that I didn't pass the eye test.

Jumbo didn't say anything outright at the time, but his body language was totally dismissive—he was even a little disrespectful—and the whole conversation was about how I was nothing special. How bigger runners get hurt too often, never perform to their potential. As expected, when I got back home, I was informed he would not be offering me a scholarship. At 17, it felt like my dream was crumbling right in front me. I was shocked that someone was against me. There were star runners on that team that wanted me there, but because I was a little taller, my legs a little thicker, my chest a little stouter than the "ideal" runner's body, it was a "no." Frankly, I was devastated.

And I learned in that moment that disappointment is an essential part of this game. Not everyone is going to like you. Not everyone is going to believe in you. And just because you think you earned it, doesn't make it real. You don't realize at the time but the pain makes you stronger—it builds the "callusing effect" that builds up your tolerance to future pain. I knew the feeling physically, but was just starting to learn about it emotionally.

So instead of feeling sorry for myself, I just ran that much harder. I tore up the New York high school record book my senior year. In April, when I ran the 2-mile in nine flat, Jumbo finally called back. But by then, still hurt, I had moved on.

Coach Frank Gagliano at Manhattan College had been recruiting me aggressively. I had a good rapport with "Gags" and it seemed like a natural fit. They had a tremendous recruiting class that year—seven guys who had run 4:15 or faster in high school. Manhattan was just across the street from Van Cortland Park so Gagliano had ample opportunities to see my unusual frame in action, and he liked what he saw. Bielen approved since it had a solid track program, but also because it too was a Christian Brotherhood institution. One of the older Power runners who I looked up to—John Lovett— was on the team. Some of the great New York distance runners I had looked up to when I was younger ended up there: Pete Squires, Mike Keogh. Fred Dwyer was still the head coach then, and he had been Marty Liquori's high school coach, so he clearly knew something about training distance runners. That indoor season they beat Villanova to win the NCAAs. It felt like poetic justice.

CHAPTER FIVE: MANHATTAN

With Brother Bielen's blessing I committed to Manhattan. It felt like the best choice in April when I was a regionally-known runner with a 4:13 mile. Instead of working at the deli that summer, I was invited to the junior national team and embarked on three weeks of travel to invitational races across the country. It was my very first time in an airplane and the beginning of a lifestyle that wouldn't stop for a decade.

On the plane before take-off, Bielen turned to me and said, "Now is as good a time as any for what I'm about to tell you." He was never shy to give advice, but somehow this felt different. Like it was something he'd been thinking about for a while, saving for this moment.

"I want you to know two things before you graduate. Number 1, in college you shouldn't drink beer."

I nodded.

He paused for what felt like an eternity. I feel like it's a stand-off, like the day he accepted me to Power. This time I finally crack, "Okay, so what's the second thing?"

"When you get married and have children, put your medals away." His language is precise, planned. He knows I come from a broken home. I never had to tell him the details. He put it all together.

"Well, don't worry," I said, "Because I'm not getting married and having children anyways."

"Well, if you do, and I hope you do, put the medals away."

It was ridiculous. I had told him directly plenty of times. I never wanted to be a parent. Even If I got married, I wouldn't have children. Everything I had experienced in life so far, I had no desire to inflict that onto someone new. But it irked me--I had to ask. "Okay, why is that? Why put the medals away?"

He calmly replied: "Trust me. There is no better feeling than a child surpassing their parent."

He of course had neither a wife nor children. So how could he know? Was he really talking about me and my future children, or me and him? I never asked.

***

The first stop was the Keebler Invitational in Chicago. Bielen and I stayed at his old high school on the south side in one of the vacant brother's rooms. We spent most of the time with Bielen's old friends in the brotherhood, but one afternoon I persuaded him to go down to the Chicago lakefront. I jumped in the water and was shocked at how cold it was even in the middle of summer. When I jumped into the water, it hit me how limited my world had been. I had never even been in a lake before. My world had been NYC. I could tell then that my world was changing. I was excited to explore everything it had to offer. I wanted more. All the hard work was paying off, and I badly wanted to soak in as much as I could.

The meet director was legendary high school coach Joe Newton, who coached York High School out in the suburbs. I found out I would be racing the 2-mile against Craig Virgin, this phenom from Lebanon, Illinois, who had made it known he was going for a U.S. record attempt. The record was then held by none other than Steve Prefontaine.

Virgin picked a brutally hot day for the attempt. It was over 90 degrees on the track, and high humidity. I was sweating hours before the race even started. The meet had an opening ceremony before the race started, and I remember watching it from under the shade of a tree, trying to stay out of the sun.

And as I'm watching I look down to the ceremony and see Craig Virgin himself, in the blazing sun, holding the American flag out in front as he lead the procession.

I could tell then a guy with that kind of confidence was going to be hard to beat. I figured with the heat it would be a slower pace and I could hang with him. I wasn't tested at the 2-mile yet and this would be a good test. But he went out hard and just kept going. The crowd knew he was going for the record and started building in excitement the third lap. By the last lap they were going crazy. He fed off their energy and seemed to grow stronger even as I was suffering far behind him in the punishing heat. Even though I ran a personal best of 8:56 he blew me—and the national record—away with an 8:40.9.

I learned a lot from Craig that day. On any given day, regardless of the environment or the circumstance, you have to stay focused on one thing: just compete. Today as a coach I hear so much about "not being in the right race" or "not being in the fast section." Sometimes it's "it's too hot," other times, "it's too cold." The list goes on. Craig went out, in punishing heat, and didn't give it a second thought. It takes immense courage to put yourself on the line, but why else do we train?

I honestly think some runners want an excuse to fall back on. I understand the temptation. It's a very human impulse. It's easier to fall short with some misplaced sense that it was out of your hands than to accept the fact that you are only as good as your results. But winning is not about things coming easily, even for the very best runners. It's about training harder and becoming mentally stronger.

The next stop was the Golden West Invitational in Sacramento the following weekend. It had only been around for 13 years but was already the most prestigious prep meet in the country. Past winners included Liquori, Ryun, long-jump great Bob Beamon, and plenty of others. Winning here would be a dream ending to my high school career.

The day before the meet they had a beauty contest of local girls—the winning girl would hand out the medals to the winners the next day. They had the medals all on display, and a lot of the runners were hitting on the girls there. I hung back and Bielen teased me, "Don't you want to talk to them?" I gave my typical New York answer: "I'll be talking to the winner after the race on Saturday, so don't you worry."

I took first in the mile in 4:08 and then doubled back less than an hour later and finished third in the 2-mile in 8:56—the exact same time here on tired legs that I ran on fresh ones in Chicago. It made me realize just how fantastic Craig's accomplishment had been. I'm convinced that in this better weather, he would have run even faster.

I put myself through a mental drill after that Golden West double that I still use with my athletes today. I added my mile and two mile times together to get a sense of what that would be for the 3-mile. 13:05. I was getting a lot of smoke blown up my ass about how good a double I had just completed, which normally I resisted. But this time I let myself enjoy it a little. And getting that medal from the beauty contest winner didn't hurt.

The next day the local paper did a write-up on my performance in the Invitational and incidentally carried the results of the NCAA Championships held down in Baton Rouge on the same day. Still full of myself but curious I glanced at the times. Prefontaine won the 3-mile (his fourth NCAA title in a row, and setting a meet record that stands today) at 13:04.0. With rest in between and adding my two times up I still wouldn't have beat Pre. So, yeah, I had some work to do.

This was my first time on the west coast. Sacramento was beautiful, warm but no humidity, and even more striking to me: it seemed like all the girls there were so fit. I asked out that beauty queen after the meet and found she was just as star-struck by me as I was by her. We got along really well. I only saw her for a couple days but we exchanged letters for months after that. I liked the girl, but I also loved hearing about life in California—and saw how fascinated she was about my life in the Bronx. For my whole life I was a New York guy surrounded by New York guys, but for the first time I was starting to realize that in the rest of the country this was a novelty to people. They liked my accent, my slang, my mannerisms.

After California, I flew to Gainesville, Florida, and won the mile in 4:02.7, the New York state high school record (still standing). An even bigger world opened up for me and, yes, maybe a couple more girls, or, maybe a few more than a couple. It was then I realized how hard it was going back to the Bronx was going to be. Over that summer, I had seen another world. More importantly, I was starting to discover a different part of me -- more confident, and more risk oriented. I had gotten a taste of something different, but after a whirlwind summer, the Bronx felt like it had just stood still - it was as if I never left.

Here I was, the #1 high school miler, finally a real name on the national running scene, and I was going to college just a few blocks from my mother's house. Still seeing all the old shady friends from the neighborhood, sleeping with the same neighborhood girls. Sure I was living in the dorm, but it still felt like I hadn't gone anywhere.

And then, after seven years without laying an eye on him, I ran into my father.

I was in a bodega one day buying a soda and came out to see a big Cadillac across the street. My father always liked big cars, even when he couldn't afford them. The car was parked on the curb, but the driver was in there, his arm out the window. My father always had a unique way of putting his arm up on the side of the car with his fingers up, holding onto the roof as if it might blow off in a stiff wind. He was a big man, 250 pounds, 5'11 or so, and looked a lot like Jackie Gleason. And I said, "God, that's just the way my father would hold the car."

I walked across the street and circled the car. I wasn't 100% sure at first—as I said, it had been seven years—then I looked in. It was him, alright. A little older, a little heavier. But that was Sid Centrowitz, no question. Would he recognize me? I was a boy last time he laid eyes on me. Now I was a big, athletic man, with long hair and mustache. I gave it a shot. I stuck my hand in the car and said, "Hey, how you doing?"

He looked startled. "Do I know you?

Just then, in one of those acts of fate, a cop shows up. I'm about to confront my father after years of fantasizing about just this very moment. I'd make up scenarios, run it over in my head 1000 times. Would I hug him? Yell at him? Punch him? My heart was racing and it was finally about to happen and suddenly, here's this traffic cop.

"You can't park here, buddy. Move it."

My father nodded, but looked back over at me. Did he recognize me? There was something in his eyes. Maybe it was there. Maybe it was my wishful thinking. Or maybe it's memory playing tricks on me. But he said to me, "I'll be right back."

He started the engine, eased the car into traffic, and drove down the street. I waited there an hour and a half.

He never came back.

***

Frustrated by the familiar surroundings, the sense that I hadn't really gone anywhere, I struggled from day one at Manhattan. I felt uninspired, running on the same tracks and against the same guys I beat in high school. I already proved I was #1, so why do it again? It completely took my edge off.

My family was so poor I was 90% on a BEOG (Basic Educational Opportunity Grant), with my athletic scholarship covering the other 10%. So, for first time since I was 13 I didn't have to work. But even with that extra time I just couldn't be bothered to try in class. They signed me up for business classes, which I found I hated. I was barely passing, barely staying eligible.

I was sleepwalking through freshman year, wondering if this is what I worked so hard for. Even the team around me didn't seem motivated. We qualified as a team to compete in the NCAA Cross-Country meet that fall, but the only ones who wanted to attend were Pete Squires (a senior) and me, who also qualified as individuals. Even Coach Dwyer didn't bother to fly out with us.

So, in a sour mood, I fly to Spokane with Pete for the NCAA Cross-Country Championships. The race was held on a golf course in Hangman Valley, a little south of town, but we stayed in town. The first night there we head to the Old Spaghetti Factory for dinner. Pete and I sit down in a booth to order and then suddenly Pete kicks me under the table.

"Pete, what the hell?"

"Matt. Behind you. Don't turn all at once. It's Prefontaine."

Sure enough, Pre and the rest of the Oregon Ducks were sitting at a long table with their coach Bill Dellinger, who had recently taken over from the legendary Bill Bowerman.

"Pete," I said, "Come on. You're a senior—act like it. It's not a bunch of rock stars over there. Remember, we're in this race too. We're just as good as them."

Pete nodded, unconvinced.

In truth, the Ducks were about as close to rock stars as existed in the running world. They were faster, cooler, more confident, always a step ahead—not just on the course or the track but in tactics or training or the newest shoes. They were the track equivalent of that team I idolized growing up: the Yankees. I played it cool in front of Pete, but I badly wanted to be accepted by the Oregon guys.

At Manhattan, we were competing mostly against other private, Catholic schools in the Northeast. Loyola, Fordham, Fairfield, Iona. The Oregon guys were competing with—and beating—the big, glamour schools of the Pac-8. UCLA—where I had watched Power Memorial alum Kareem Abdul-Jabar dominate on the court. University of Washington. Stanford. Cal. Stanford. USC. These were big-time programs. Big time athletes. And in a time when it felt like New York City was coming apart, like it was the old world passing away before our eyes, the West Coast felt like the future. I kept thinking back to that first trip to California and that tan, long-legged beauty queen from Sacramento. From that moment on the West had grabbed hold of me as some sort of breezy, confident new world, and I wanted to be a part of it.

After we finished our food, I dragged the star-struck Pete over to their table and we introduced ourselves. They welcomed us to sit with them. Nice guys. But their elite status was unspoken. It's almost like they were too confident, they didn't need a chip on their shoulder. When they invited us to work out with them the next day, I accepted with as much nonchalance as I could muster. Honestly I think they realized we were there alone without our team or even our coach and just felt bad for us.

The next morning, we arrive at their hotel. We knock on the door of Terry Williams, then their number two runner behind Pre, and Pre opens the door, shirtless. Pete's eyes bug out of his head, but he doesn't say anything. Later he's elbowing me, saying under his breath "Did you see that barrel chest, man?" He was so shameless I couldn't help but laugh.

Dellinger met us out in the lobby and drove us out to the course. He was a three-time Olympian, running in 1956, 1960, and 1964, and brought home the Bronze in the 5000m at the Tokyo Olympics in '64. By then, he was almost 40 years old, more than double my age, but to my total shock he didn't just drive us to the course, he stripped down to his shorts and ran with us.

"Your coach always run with you?" I asked Dave Taylor, one of their better runners.

"Yeah, why" he replied with a smile, "Your coach never run with you?"

Pete of course clung to Pre the whole time, but I was much more interested in Dellinger. I had read all about his predecessor, Bill Bowerman, the now-legendary coach who took over in Oregon in the 1940s, went on to win 5 NCAA Championships, produce dozens of All-Americans, and eventually would become the head coach for Team USA Track and Field in the 1972 Olympics. (He was also co-founder of a then-little-known shoe company called Blue Ribbon Sports which would later change its name to Nike.)

I'd heard of Dellinger but didn't know much specifically about him. But I knew enough about Oregon to know that anybody good enough to take over from Bowerman without so much as a slight dip in performance from that team had to be good. So, while Pete ran with the pack up ahead, I jogged next to Dellinger and started hitting him with blunt questions. And to his credit he hit me right back with blunt answers.

"Coach Dellinger, I got a question."

"Don't call me coach. Just Bill. Call me Bill."

That was a new one, but as I would later learn, a key part of the culture at Oregon.

"Uh... Bill. So why didn't you recruit me?"

He shrugged. "I really didn't know you."

I ran the fastest high school mile in the country that year. He didn't know me?

"Bill, you think I can make All-American?" (All-American would require placing 25th or better in the race the next day.)

"Nope."

"How come?"

"You're not fast enough."

How would he know, if he didn't know me?

I kept feeling him out, man to man. Not trying to suck up to him but showing him my seriousness, my focus, my drive. Whatever he thought of me, he didn't show it.

I decided this race wasn't just going to be about hitting a PR, or making All-American. It was going to be about showing I could be runner for Oregon. But more important than showing Dellinger or Terry Williams or even Pre, it was about showing myself. If I could hang with these guys, as a freshman, then I'd know that's where I really belonged. If they blew me away, maybe Manhattan was all I could ever aspire to. Suddenly that fire, that inner motivation, that had been missing all season came surging back. I couldn't wait to race the next day.

After we got back from the course jog, we headed over to a mandatory technical meeting. The event organizers made a big deal about how bad the traffic was going to be from the city down to Hangman Valley and how imperative it was for us to leave extremely early to beat that traffic. Pete Squires agreed and we planned to leave the next morning at 5am—for an 11am race.

While we were there, we were supposed to go into a storage room and take an NCAA meet t-shirt. Pete and I head in and suddenly he says, "Let's take a box." I think, okay, I could take three for four extra shirts for my brother and some friends maybe, but just as I'm figuring this out Pete runs out of the room with the entire box of over 100 shirts. I follow him back to the hotel, and instead of running up to our room he camps out in the lobby and starts questioning runners as they file in.

"Hey, d'you get a T-shirt?"

Invariably they'd answer "No, they ran out of shirts for some reason."

"No problem," Pete would say, "I've got an extra."

So, he spent that afternoon slinging T-shirts like he was bestowing papal favors. For the life of me I couldn't understand what he was doing. Why bother stealing the shirts if you were just going to give them back to the guys? Later I asked why on earth he did it. His answer? "When you're from New York people expect you to do something outlandish. It comes with the territory." On that count, Pete delivered.

***

The next morning, we were up at 5am and started our shakeout run. It was late November by this point and easily below freezing at that point in the day. We get to the course and you can guess how many other idiots are there as early as us: yep, zero. We're the only ones dumb enough to show up five hours early.

"There aren't even lines painted on the damn course yet!" I told Pete.

"So what," he said, "We warm up early, we're ahead of the game."

Warm is a relative word here. The sun's still not up, the wind is blowing across the eastern Washington plains (more like tundra at that time of year), I'm hiding behind a tree trying to keep from freezing. Slowly the officials show up and I try to keep my muscles warm for hours as the rest of the field files onto the course. There was, of course, never any traffic jam.

We're joined by more and more runners, soon to be more than 200 in all. Washington State, Indiana, Western Kentucky, Tennessee, William & Mary, Massachusetts. Runners from all over. But no Oregon. As we got closer and closer to the start of the race I almost started to feel nervous—for them. How was I supposed to beat the Ducks if the Ducks weren't here?

And then, just a few minutes before the gun was scheduled to go off, this van comes racing up to the starting line. The door swings open and out jump the Oregon Ducks. They already have their spikes on, looking warm and fresh and—as always— serenely confident. They do ten warm-up strides and they are on the line. I look over at my "captain," who had me freezing my ass off for hours, and he gives me a sheepish smile. Oh well. Here we go.

Oregon was the clear favorites for the team title, and it felt like almost a given that Prefontaine would win. He had taken the title both years prior and in the final race of his collegiate career was considered a heavy favorite. When the gun went off it didn't take long for Pre and this sophomore from Western Kentucky named Nick Rose to pull away from the pack. I knew I couldn't hang with Pre, but the rest of the Ducks were fair game. So, I quickly spotted Terry Williams and Dave Taylor (Oregon's #2 and #3 guys) and latched onto them. Their pace was going to be my pace. I'd prove to myself, if nobody else, that I was fit to be a Duck.

The weather was cold but clear, and the course was dry. Terry and Dave seemed content to run a conservative pace for the first five miles—well behind the 26th man All-American cut-off. Then in the last mile they made their move, and I moved with them. Suddenly we were passing guys. I don't know if they knew I was so deliberately running with them, or if I was just another runner they had to beat. I'd never question their motivation—I know they were as hungry to perform well as anybody—but I was running for more than this race. I was running to prove I belonged, to prove to myself who I really was.

For the first and only time in a cross-country race I outkicked Dave Taylor (he would smoke me the following year) and just barely missed making All-American as a freshman, crossing the finish line in 29th place. Terry had just that much more strength and pulled away into 22nd place. Pete came in at 41st. My fellow freshman Craig Virgin took 10th. And in 1st, over a full minute faster than me, was Pre.

That night we attended the post-race banquet, which was really the first banquet of any kind I'd been to in my life. The room was packed with runners, coaches, Washington State boosters, and the like, and yet again, everybody was there early except for The Oregon Ducks. Pre had won the race the third year in a row—in fact he had not lost a single collegiate race in the 3 mile, 5,000m, 6 mile, or 10,000m. And though we all expected great things from him at the international level, this was the final chapter of his collegiate career. Oregon had won as a team, of course, their 2nd title in three years. So, if they were late, the banquet sure wasn't going to start without them.

Yet again, they arrived just in the nick of time. Dellinger and Prefontaine led the Oregon team into the room and the place went nuts. Instead of our competitors, we were treating these guys like the Rolling Stones. It was nothing I had ever seen before or since.

Pete and I were sitting in the furthest corner of the room, at a table with a couple of other orphaned runners without their coaches or team. At the end of the banquet the Ducks make their way out as a group, but Dellinger veered off over to my table and stopped. To my great surprise he shook my hand and said, "You ran one hell of a race. Especially without a team and a coach here for you. Keep it up." And then, before I could muster anything smart in response, he walked out.

Coach Dwyer didn't even bother to call me.

***

When I got back to New York I told Brother Bielen about my determination to transfer to Oregon. He supported my ambition but pointed out a couple of obstacles. First, if I transferred without my current coach's permission I'd lose a year of eligibility. I'd be ineligible to compete for a full year. Second, my grades were much too poor. With a 1.8 I was barely staying eligible at Manhattan, and far from the 2.5 I'd need to transfer. I also didn't have the money to fly myself to Oregon. And then, he reminded me, Dellinger might not even want me.

I wrote Dellinger a letter and told him I wanted nothing more than to be on the Oregon team. His advice was blunt and honest as ever: "We have never had a transfer make it here. And I understand people typically transfer because they are unhappy and they have learned bad habits in their current environment. My advice is to stay at Manhattan and work out your current problems." And yet, he didn't say no.

Brother Bielen read the response and told me if I got my grades up and transferred he'd pay for my plane ticket. So, I knew I had my objective. I changed my major to PE and took easier classes like First Aid. I pushed myself through the indoor and outdoor track seasons at Manhattan with a newfound focus.

And by spring I had pulled my average back up to 2.5 and formally applied to transfer to Oregon.

The response I got from Dellinger was night and day from the first one. "I'm happy you're coming to Oregon."

Coach Gags was supportive—he too was out the door for a head coaching job at Rutgers. But Dwyer wouldn't budge. I found out later that Dwyer and Dellinger were actually good friends, dating back to their days as Olympic runners in the 50s. And my choice to transfer to Oregon led to a rift between the two that would last for years.

Because Dwyer wouldn't release me, if I transferred I'd be back to my old meat delivery status—practicing but not competing—for a full year.

I didn't even hesitate.

CHAPTER SIX: EUGENE

True to his word, Brother Bielen paid for my one-way plane ticket to Oregon. I said goodbye to my mother, my brother, the neighborhood friends I had, and my teammates. If going from Power to Manhattan felt like too small a step forward, Oregon was a huge leap into the unknown. As badly as I wanted to be there, Oregon felt like another planet from New York. I was 3,000 miles from everyone I knew in the world, and too broke for a return plane ticket.

After a whole day of flying (New York to Chicago to Eugene, I get to the airport with all my belongings in the world, looking forward to finally seeing Dellinger after all these months. All I see is this one young guy standing around, waiting for somebody. In case he's with Bill I walk up to him and introduce myself.

"You're Centrowitz?" he says, "No offense, but I expected a small, skinny distance runner."

"I'm sorry, too," I said, "Because I expected Bill Dellinger."

The guy—who turned out to be a graduate assistant—laughed. "You think Bill is picking up a transfer at the airport? Time to adjust your expectations."

It stung but I got it. Right now I was nobody special.

Bill headed the running department of an all-sports camp in Seaside, Oregon that summer, and had invited me out early. Seaside is a tiny beach town on the Oregon coast that swells with weekenders in the summer and goes back to being a sleepy burg in the off-season. I was the only Oregon runner Bill had invited there, and as a result we began what would become a very close relationship over those weeks. He would give me personalized workouts every day, and paid close attention to my times. His knowledge of me as a runner and as a person started right there on the Oregon coast.

One day he drove me ten miles outside of camp into the forested hills that line the coast. Whatever logging road he had chosen, it was a desolate one. I didn't see a single car, pedestrian, horse, nothing - the whole drive out. The gray Pacific mist hung over the trees, and the sky above the ocean was dark, threatening rain. I could run through the roughest parts of the Bronx no problem, but this wilderness was starting to make me nervous.

"What's up in these hills, Bill? Any animals?"

"Oh yeah," he said, his face blank, "This is wild country out here. Plenty of cougars."

"Wait, what the hell is a cougar?"

"Kind of a mountain lion."

Mountain lions are definitely not what I signed up for.

"Bear, too. But they're harmless, if you play dead. Mountain lion you'll have to outrun."

And then he dropped me off.

"Why don't you jog a half-mile down the road and back and then we'll start you off."

He handed me a wrist-watch with a timer on it. I jogged my warmup and then ran back to the car.

"Okay, are you ready?"

Just then the sky opens up and it starts to rain hard. I'm soaked in seconds. He starts to drive away. I run after him, yelling and waiving my hands. He stops and rolls down the window just a crack.

"Yeah, Rube, what do you want?"

"Is there any way for me to be a champion besides this?"

He didn't answer. Just laughed, shook his head, and drove off.

Imagining a pack of mountain lions on my tail, I ran back to camp as fast as I could.

***

I didn't totally understand it when I transferred, but Oregon track was in a state of transition. Bill Bowerman, who had coached for 25 years, had abruptly retired without warning, just a few months before I met Dellinger. Their transcendent star, Prefontaine, graduated that winter and would tragically be killed in a car accident just over a year later. Dellinger was stepping into the enormous shadow of Bowerman and doing so without—after that final race where I met him—Bowerman's ace.

As if symbolizing this transitional time, storied Hayward Field itself was under construction. The grandstand had been torn down and was being rebuilt—with the hope of the improved facility hosting the 1976 Olympic Trials. Was I arriving at the end of an era, or the beginning of a new one?

Another thing I could never have anticipated was how much Oregon's success and casual sense of confidence was rooted in the community around the school. It seemed mind-blowing to me, but these people in and around Eugene truly loved running. In New York people came to the meets because there was nothing better to do. Out in Oregon, it was a religion. They treated all of us, not just the stars, like we were something special. Eugene calls itself Track Town USA, and there's not even a close second place.

I loved that aspect of it, but Eugene was also—especially then—about as different from New York City as you could find in America at the time. I was used to going to discos, blow-drying my hair, wearing bell-bottoms and platform shoes. I would wear cologne and iron my clothes before going out. But Eugene was still living the end of the hippy dream, it was grunge before grunge even existed. Flannels and baggy pants. Girls didn't shave their legs or their armpits. Guys would skip showers for days. And it's not like these kids were poor—it was just an attitude. I never saw anything like it.

Over the course of the summer and the early fall, Bill's attention and tough love shaped me into a stronger runner, both physically and mentally. Even though I had proved to be one of the fastest guys on the team, Bill followed the tradition passed down by Hayward and Bowerman and put me in the JV locker room. If the personal attention that summer had built up any feeling of being special, this JV status brought me back down to earth.

At Oregon, JV status made it clear what you were:

Varsity Locker Room	JV Locker Room
Located immediately on the right when you walk in the door.	Stuck at the very end of the long hallway.
One door down from the showers, so you only had to walk for a very short time on the cold cement to get to the shower.	Very far from the showers, so you spent a long time walking on the cold cement to and from the showers. Very cold in the winter.
Carpeted	Cold tile
On the entry door, there was a big logo "Fighting Ducks" Men of Oregon	Nothing on the wall
Inside: chin up bar and full-length Duck-green lockers	Half lockers, bright yellow.
Personalized lockers. That's where the coaches would put your personalized training logs!	No names on any of the lockers. You know why? You didn't matter. You didn't earn your name yet.
ONLY varsity athletes allowed.	Shared the locker room with OTC members.
Brand new Duck-green workout gear, nobody in the country had this stuff, embroidered with U of O logo, hooded sweatshirt.	Prison gray shorts and t-shirt, hoodless sweatshirt stamped with "I.U." – intramural. And it was a year old. It had been used before. We didn't matter.

But strangely, I've given or thrown away almost every uniform I had. The varsity uniform I eventually earned. My Team USA Olympic uniform. But the one thing I've kept to this day is that gray hoodless University of Oregon JV sweatshirt.

I loved that varsity green, though. I wanted it so bad. But I embraced the challenge. If this is what it takes, I'm all in. All the rest is ego. I was plenty used to pain at that point. That JV locker room was dingy but there were peoples' homes in the Bronx that were much worse. I think we've gotten too far away from this as American runners today. We've lost that discomfort and sacrifice. Our elite talents get treated like they have elite achievements before they've even done it. Runners from developing countries often seem hungrier—they've embraced the discomfort and pain that too many of our athletes now avoid.

Throughout this first year, even though I was treated like nothing special at workouts, an unspoken bond started to develop between me and Bill. He didn't take it easy on me— he was never one to play favorites. But as much as I craved approval and mentorship, he seemed willing to give it.

Like a lot of great athletes and coaches, Bill was hyper-competitive, even in matters far from the track. He never played a game just for fun—he had to win. Once we made a bet about my hair—he had insisted for months that I cut it, but I wanted to look cool and keep it long. We settled on a "best of three" games of pool at 5pm Friday in the student union. If I won, I would keep my hair long and he'd never mention it again. If I lost I would have to shave it.

The word spread about our bet, so the entire team showed up. Almost 50 runners and field event guys came out, all rooting me on to shut Bill up. I'm ready, I'm focused, I'm warmed up. And Bill, uncharacteristically, shows up 15 minutes late.

I offered him a chance to warm up but he declined. "Since I'm late, I forfeit my warmup. Only fair." Strangely passive of him. So, I offered him the chance to break. And he declined again.

So, we started. I broke and shot three balls in. And then on his first turn he ran the table. Uh oh. The second game he does the same exact thing, sweeping the rack in a single turn. I look up and see my large adoring crowd has dispersed. I was toast.

Bill smiled and said to me "See you in my office at 9am Monday for your haircut."

Later he admitted to me that his tardiness was pure gamesmanship. He had been across the street at a bar warming up with games of pool and cocktails for over an hour before our match. I didn't realize it, but by the time I broke the first game, I was already doomed.

Another time, I kidded him for being a little flabby at the age of 40. He still ran workouts with us—which none of my previous coaches ever did—but he was getting into middle age, and obviously his body wasn't the same as the 20-year-old All-Americans running next to him.

He asked, "You think you're going to be in that kinda shape at 40, Matt?"

At that age 40 seemed as far away as 100. But, if I kept running, why not? "Of course."

"Okay," he said, "I'll make you a bet. When you're 40 in, what, 1995?"

"Yeah," I said. 1995 felt like science fiction, it was so far in the future.

"When you're 40 I say you'll be both fat and bald. If you're not, I owe you $100. But when you are, you owe me a hundred. Deal?"

I smiled, "You got yourself a bet, Bill."

***

I butted heads with Bill over a lot of things, but I never argued with him when it came to training. His results spoke for themselves. And so, at that point in my life, did mine.

Bowerman was the legend but Bill did more than just replicate Bowerman's system. He built on it and expanded it. The spirit of Oregon wasn't just "here's how we do things," it was a constant hunger for improvement in all aspects—training, performance, coaching, equipment, shoes, track surface, you name it.

At the heart of distance training were five core Oregon Principles, which as a coach I continue to emulate to this day:

1. **Moderation** – For college runners, it's very hard to strike a balance between hard work and recovery. Academics and the burning-the-candle-at-both-ends aspects of college life can make this even tougher. But burnout and overtraining are just as perilous as not working hard enough.

2. **Progression** - You can't scale a cliff of conditioning— you have to run up the hill. Realistic, steady progress is the key to peak performance, not throwing yourself immediately into the hardest possible workouts.

3. **Adaptation** – You must adapt your training to what you are going to face in the race. Today I continue to use the Oregon Hard-Easy system, alternating hard and easy workouts on subsequent days. This simulates the challenges of championship schedules at both the NCAA and Olympic trial levels.

4. **Variation** – The three distinct seasons—Cross-Country, Indoor, and Outdoor—offer a baseline natural variation. But it's essential to keep your body—and your brain—from falling into overly familiar routines. Avoid a training rut at all costs.

5. **Callousing** – You're not just conditioning your body. You're making yourself mentally tougher. The races you win will be the ones you've pushed yourself through pain to unfamiliar territories. Callousing yourself to pain, layer by layer, is essential.

Since I was a redshirt that first year, I wasn't getting any scholarship money, so Bill would find odd jobs for me to do. I worked that first summer at Weyerhaeuser in the graveyard shift for $5 an hour (double what I was making in the deli in the Bronx). One of the most memorable I had was painting the new stands—stands that seated almost 8,000 people, if you can imagine the scale of the job. So here I was painting the stands while guys slower than me are down on the track, eligible for competition. But did I wish I was back in Manhattan College? Not once.

***

It's ten in the morning and we had just finished the 45 minute drive from Eugene to the McKenzie River trailhead. I drove there with a couple of my new Oregon teammates. I had recently arrived in the state, my new home, and it honestly felt like the most alien place I had ever been to. I thought it would stay warm, sunny and golden through early fall, like California. Instead it was cool and moody, damp and prone to fog, a place made up of equal parts loggers, farmers and weirdo hippies. I wasn't sure I was going to like spending the next four years of my life here, especially because this first year I would not be allowed to compete. On the trip up, they told me that we would park the car at mileage marker 45 and run up the trail for 13 miles and then go back out to the highway and hitch hike back to the car. They told me I'd fall in love with this run. I would want to come back and run it again and again.

It was a beautiful crisp Pacific Northwest morning. The air smelled so fresh I could taste it. It rained some on the drive up and there were patches of thick fog; the dude driving kept talking about black ice on the road. What the fuck is black ice? As we got to the trailhead, the sky cleared to a color blue that I had never seen before. Oregon was so new to my senses;

90

everything looked and smelled different. Damn my lungs liked what they felt. All of a sudden I wasn't feeling stagnant anymore.

We stretched a little as we got out of the car, but one of the guys said we didn't have to warm up too much, since we'd start slow on the single-track trail of soft pine needles. He said my legs would thank me. As soon as we started, the full force of the place hit me, a stunningly beautiful river and surrounding forest, sounds and smells like nothing I had ever known. The run took me past old growth forest (not that I even knew what that was), waterfalls, mosses, ferns and the bluest pools of water you could ever imagine. It teased me with surprises around every bend, slowly turning a run into something new for me - a dreamlike meditation, something spiritual. Some call it flow. Others call it a runner's high. I didn't know what it was. I just knew, like Dorothy, that I wasn't in Kansas anymore.

I had no idea at the time, but this river, the McKenzie River, was intertwined with the very roots of Oregon running. The McKenzie is what brought the first legendary Oregon track coach, Bill Hayward, to the University of Oregon. He loved to fish and thought it had the best fly fishing in the world. The river in turn seduced Hayward's successor, the even more legendary Bill Bowerman, who built a home with his two hands on a bench just above the McKenzie. From that perch, he changed the world of track, started the running revolution in the country, and co-founded Nike.

Dellinger spent his high school years alongside that river, in Springfield, Oregon. He too was drawn by the inescapable attraction of the McKenzie. Just a few months ago I was still in the Bronx. Now, like them, I was falling in love. What was it about this river path that drew people, especially the track man, the runner?

Distance runners are different animals. We aren't like football or basketball players, or golfers or athletes from any other sports. We don't spend our time hitting each other, playing one-on-one or trying to make baskets, score goals, or anything else. Instead, we spend the bulk of our sports lives in solitude, lost in our thoughts. Hours and hours of training alone, our mind free, floating like a peaceful hot air balloon. Running on that magnificent trail, I found something new, like meditation, but still soaking in the beauty of the run unconsciously, almost through osmosis.

Now warmed up and used to the soft new surface, I looked up and ahead, eyes wide open to five hundred shades of green, soft browns, sharp blues. Even black looked different, from wet lava rocks trickling water to the craggy black bark of wet fir trees. I didn't know you could smell, taste and feel a run. I had logged hundreds of miles, pounding the pavement and

92

looping city parks since I was a kid, but I never knew a run could be like this.

Perhaps oddest of all for me was the way that time receded during this run. Middle distance and distance runners have a unique relationship with time. It's not just the way that the absolute numbers define your whole performance; running means nothing without splits, race times and records. It's the psychology of time itself that defines runners; how we fight with it, hide from it, and celebrate it, in secret and on our own. When a runner is focused on time ticking by, an hour run can feel like it will never end. But when we get lost in our thoughts, that same hour can fly by in a matter of seconds. Your body, like a racehorse, just wants to keep going.

Over the course of a running career, all the different kinds of time, the personal bests, world records, repeat intervals of 200's, 400's, 800's, 1200's and miles, they all lock into our heads so strongly that they become short cuts to remember telephone numbers, addresses, birthdays, passwords, etc. Times become lifetime goals, make stadiums full of fans go wild, and drive some runners crazy when they stay forever out of reach. For some of us, times can be a shortcut for a state of mind or a good memory: 3:59, 8:56; 13:12.93, for me these aren't just numbers, they bring back memories and feelings of hard work, glory or shame. But for this run, there is no time, and it feels strange.

On a run, a runner's mind is full of races he still hasn't run. Races that can be won over and over again. Fans keep cheering. Foes that have gotten the best of you are now yours – you just keep beating them and you never get tired of it. Sometime you lead from the gun, other times miraculously surging through the tape to catch them at the end. Runners' minds float free from our bodies. Scenario after scenario flows freely. Whether the cold winter air burns your skin, or the wind batters your face, it doesn't matter. Sometimes it's an evil hill that never ends, or mud and rain that poke at your confidence, but you don't give up.

The mind is what keeps it all from beating you, a different kind of training than the one that strengthens your lungs and legs. It's about building what Dellinger called the right 'temperament'. A runner's temperament is what keeps a runner steady through it all, steady because he wants to get better, because he loves to train and because he can't wait to compete. All that time, mile after mile, alone in my thoughts, was making me into somebody different than I had been, somebody I didn't quite know yet.

Little did I know then, but within in two short years, I would be running on that trail again with an Oregon team that would ultimately win a Cross Country National Championship, a team of runners from places as diverse as Cuba and Alaska, from homes where they only spoke Spanish to places like Glide, Oregon, where they only spoke country. That team had the greatest collection of American distance runners to ever compete in college. Some of us chased women, drank and stayed out late. Others were born again Christians who counted every hour of sleep and prayed to God to keep them from temptation. Even so, on that single track we were all alike. We all had the same internal rhythms, the same thoughts floating through our minds, and the same two devotions: the Oregon lime green singlet and the conquering of the clock.

On that beautiful Sunday, along that crazy river on the McKenzie Trail, I found my run. I read it somewhere, a quote from this philosopher who was obsessed with time, "Your body moves always in the present, the dividing line between the past and the future. But your mind is more free." I'm no philosopher, but for a runner, that quote always makes perfect sense to me. The runner's body trains and races, always driven by the clock. It's absolute and the runner's mind accepts it. Running has no judgment calls, no replay reviews, the racing strategies are often as simple as 'stay with him and outkick him in the last straight-away.' Physically it is not complicated. But your mind can be your greatest ally or your worst enemy. The runner's mind makes us different. For us, time is absolute, as is victory or defeat. We live with the clarity of time, and because of this, the runner's mind is ultimately more free.

CHAPTER SEVEN: MEN OF OREGON

From 1903 until 1998, Oregon had three track and field coaches, and they were all named Bill. The last one turned out to be my best friend and mentor. He taught me not only how to coach, but more importantly, how to be a man. It was from him, in his own understated way, that I learned how Oregon grew to become the program that it was.

To me, Oregon was like the Yankees of my childhood, one of those great sports programs that is about so much more than their win/loss record, the stadiums, the fans, or even the athletes. Instead, what makes the great programs great is the culture they create. A culture that touches and pulls in everyone who enters its orbit. There's no formula for this. It's something that happens organically – like members of a hive, who all think they are operating as individuals but instead are serving some bigger destiny.

The Oregon culture was unique, the creation of a few outsized individuals building something from scratch out on the western frontier.

Bill Hayward was Oregon's first coach. He was a gifted multisport athlete who grew up in Toronto. At the turn of the century, he left behind a career racing for thousands of dollars in cash to become a college coach, first at Princeton, then at Berkeley. A passionate fly fisherman, a chance vacation took him to Oregon and he fell in love, leaving a plum job at the crown jewel of the University of California system to sign on as the coach of Pacific University, a tiny college in the Willamette Valley south of Portland. Three years later, he was offered the job at the University of Oregon. He took it and never left the state, spending the next 44 years as the head track coach and head athletic trainer for Oregon.

Hayward's accomplishments were legendary: four world record holders; six American record holders and nine Olympic team members. Six times he was selected to be on the staff of the American team for the Olympic Games. He even coached Jim Thorpe at the 1912 Stockholm Olympics. He was so popular that, less than halfway through his coaching tenure, the University named its new football field 'Hayward Field'. And all this in a state that was just a generation removed from the Old West.

In 44 years of coaching, Hayward put together some of the best track teams of the era, but just as importantly, he stoked a passion for track in the community. Thousands of Oregonians, many of whom had never gone to the University of Oregon—or any college—came out to support his teams, and the special love affair between community and the sport of track started with him.

In 1929, Bill Hayward was taping the ankles of a young football player from eastern Oregon named Bill Bowerman, when that younger Bill asked, "I hear people call you Colonel."

"Just call me Bill," was Hayward's response, a simple, straightforward approach that would be repeated again and again over the next 60 years. The next season, Bowerman joined the track team, ultimately returning to Hayward field to succeed Hayward as coach in 1948 - after serving in combat in the Italian alps as part of an elite ski patrol.

During his tenure, his athletes won 24 NCAA individual titles and 4 NCAA team championships. His teams also had 33 Olympians, 38 conference champions and 64 All-Americans. In 1972, his final year at Oregon, he served as the head track coach of the U.S. Olympic team and played a vital—if controversial—role in protecting American athletes during the crisis in Munich.

Bowerman was more than just a great coach. He thought of himself as a teacher and an innovator. Like his last name, which means "builder man" in German, he was someone that was most interested in building a program and making its people and sports products better. Everything about him was built on a philosophical foundation.

Forty years after Bowerman met Hayward, when I showed up to the Oregon locker room, I heard the same thing, "Just call me Bill." Dellinger, the third in a line of great Bills, was my coach, a quiet, rough-hewn guy from Springfield, Eugene's blue collar sister, and one of the greatest distance runners to ever come out of the state.

I guess that phrase, "Just call me Bill" sticks with me to this day because of what it says about the humility (and the lack of pretense) that formed the foundation of Oregon track. It ties together coach and athlete, track program and community. I still don't know how it all came together, but in 1974, I walked into a team, and a town, with its own code, traditions built over decades by men who were a lot tougher and had seen a lot more than this young guy from the Bronx.

Bill told me more than once about how, before every season, Bowerman would gather his freshman and give his famous "Men of Oregon" speech. Kenny Moore, an Oregon runner who went on to become a terrific writer at *Sports Illustrated*,

100

did a great job telling the story of his own first experience with "the speech." In his version, Bowerman stood up in front of that year's recruits and said:

> Men of Oregon, take a primitive organism,
> any weak, pitiful organism. Say a freshman.
> Make it lift, or jump or run. Let it rest. What
> happens? A little miracle. It gets a little
> better. It gets a little stronger or faster or
> more enduring. That's all training is. Stress.
> Recover. Improve. You'd think any damn
> fool could do it.

Bowerman went on to describe how athletes always overdo it by overtraining, or getting hurt or being irresponsible and flunking out. He gave a parable that communicated a second foundational principle at Oregon. Again, from Kenny Moore's great book:

> Farmer can't get his mule to plow. Can't
> even get him to eat or drink. Finally calls in
> a mule skinner. Guy comes out, doesn't
> even look at the mule. Goes in the barn,
> gets a two-by-four and hits the mule as
> hard as he can between the ears. Mule
> goes to his knees. Mule skinner hits him

again, between the eyes. Farmer drags him off.

"That's supposed to get him to plow? That's supposed to get him to drink?"

"I can see you don't know a damn thing about mules", says the skinner. "First you have to get their attention"'

Bill Bowerman knew, and he taught Bill Dellinger, that before you could coach you had to first get the athlete's attention. Sometimes he'd just grab an athlete gently but firmly by the neck until he could tell they were listening. Brick by brick, Bowerman built on the foundation that Hayward had left for him - keeping his athletes healthy, emphasizing moderation in training, focusing on technique. To that, Bowerman added a greater emphasis on competing intelligently, and most importantly, focusing on the athletes that were the most eager, rather than the athletes that had the most talent. He once said, "If you have a body, you are an athlete." His greatest interest was in working with the athletes that just wanted to get better, regardless of how talented they were.

Some of Bowerman's maxims ended up as the foundation for the "Oregon Way", and these sawhorses were passed down to me (and everybody else) by Dellinger:

102

The idea that the harder you work, the better you're going to be is just garbage. The greatest improvement is made by the man or woman who works most intelligently.

I want you to finish every workout exhilarated, not exhausted.

The real purpose of running isn't to win a race, it's to test the limits of the human heart.

Victory is in having done your best. If you've done your best you've won.

A teacher is never too smart to learn from his pupils.

If you have a body, you are an athlete.

The hay's in the barn.

Bowerman was a towering figure, but my Bill was perhaps the ultimate distillation of what Oregon Track was really about. Not just because he was a hometown boy who became one of the best distance runners to ever run for the University of

Oregon (and the U.S.), but because he grew up in that culture, because he *was* Oregon track.

Once he retired as an athlete, after the 1964 Olympic Games, Dellinger signed on as an assistant track coach under Bowerman and began his apprenticeship. He helped Bowerman coach some of the greatest Oregon distance runners through the late 60's until he finally became head track and cross country coach in 1972 and started bringing along a young kid from Coos Bay that ended up defining Oregon for generations of track fans.

Dellinger was a great athlete, winning numerous NCAA titles, setting World and American records and running the 5k in the 1956, 1960 and 1964 Olympic Games, finally medaling in 1964 in Tokyo. To me, though, he was an even better coach and better man than he was an athlete, and everything I learned about running, or coaching, I learned from him.

When I transferred from Manhattan College and spent the summer in Eugene, I will never forget going to my first official cross country meeting. Bill asked us all to show up at 3pm at the Hayward Field west grandstands. There, he gave us his own version of the "Men of Oregon" speech. I don't know if it was just as Bill Bowerman gave it, but I do know that it hit me. I knew I was a part of something special.

Somehow, just like that meeting, I can still picture our first cross country practice. There had to have been over 100 runners there, literally a 100 runners. They were all there, in different groups doing repeat miles around the old cinder track next to Hayward Field. I was in shock. It made no sense to me how Oregon could have that many guys on the Cross Country team.

I found out later that Dellinger allowed literally anyone to try out for the team. It was hard for me to believe that the most successful cross country team in the country had completely open tryouts. However, at Oregon, if you had a body you were an athlete. It was the Oregon Way. And Dellinger, like his mentor Bowerman, and like Bowerman's mentor, Hayward, was always the most interested in the guys that just wanted to get better, not the ones who were most talented. Anyone interested in trying to make the Oregon team was welcome to try.

The Bills of Oregon built a culture that was all about being real. Yes, it was about winning, setting records, having the greatest fans and volunteers in the world, but mostly, it was about being real, being honest, and doing your best. I've heard that Phil Knight, a former Oregon runner and co-founder (with Bill Bowerman) of Nike – now one of the most powerful people in sports, has always insisted that his employees just call him Phil.

He doesn't like being addressed as Mr. Knight. "Just call me, Bill" helped shape him and he took those lessons and spread them throughout his company.

Almost as soon as I arrived, Bowerman and Dellinger had a bad falling out. It was a mystery to a lot of people why it happened and why it was never fully repaired. But after that split, Dellinger lost a lot of support. I took this personally, and so did a bunch of other guys on the team. Bill Dellinger was our coach and we loved him. Even at a special place like Oregon, things don't always go smoothly. And although the Bowerman-Dellinger split was never fully reconciled, the culture that Hayward, Bowerman and Dellinger built was bigger than any one man. That's what makes a culture like that so powerful— it may have started with Hayward and gotten famous with Pre, but it has thrived beyond any single figure. You can have rips in certain places, but in the end, the cultural fabric stays strong and keeps bringing more and more people comfort and direction.

"Just call me, Bill" stands for so much more than those simple few words.

***

Before I got to Oregon, it never occurred to me that I was missing a father figure in my life, or more importantly, that I needed someone who could be both father and friend. I didn't exactly come to Oregon looking for that, I thought I just wanted to see something different in the world and to be part of a cool program. But underneath my tough Bronx hide, what I wanted more than anything else was someone that I could look up to, who would help guide me. Maybe I sensed that Dellinger could be that guy, but I don't think it was anything conscious that drove me to Oregon. But it was in Eugene that I finally found the father I never had – a guy who would love me for who I was, who saw through all my bullshit. It took me a while to believe in that love - I didn't want to be abandoned like I was when I was a kid, left waiting on a curb for a father that would never return. But at some point during that first year at Oregon, I started to realize that Bill would always be there for me.

We were an odd 'family', that's for sure. I was from the Bronx. He grew up in Grants Pass, Oregon, which was truly *country*. He then spent his high school years in Springfield, which was also *country*. As a kid, before his PE teacher discovered his distance running talent, he hung out with much older guys, smoking cigarettes and chasing girls.

Bill was country. I was the Bronx. He loved the outdoors, especially hunting for musk-rats and fishing for trout. I thought the *outdoors* was nothing more than going outside. He listened to Willie Nelson and Johnny Cash. I liked Peter Frampton and Billy Joel. Dressing up for him was cowboy boots; for me it was John Travolta's platforms in Saturday Night Fever. We couldn't have been more different.

However, there was something about him that made the relationship such a natural one. I don't know if it was his self-confidence, or his straight up, no-bullshit way of talking to people. I wanted to be like him, and for some reason he seemed to like me from the very start. Underneath all those differences, we were a lot alike. Bill enjoyed having a beer or two, and we both often carried a bit of extra weight from drinking. Like me, he liked women and I think they liked him even more. But even though he stayed out, drank, gambled and was popular with women, he never missed a workout. Once I had graduated from Oregon, a guy we called "the Colonel" (a runner from Kentucky, Michael Haywood, who is still one of my best friends) and I used to hang out with him at the Vet's club. That's when he started letting me into his life off the track, and our friendship became a deeper one.

Bill was simple, but not simplistic. When he was a runner, he counted his intervals by sticking his fingers out so that he wouldn't lose count. When he talked to his athletes about intervals, he used the same finger-counting method to tell you exactly what you had to do. Like Bowerman and Hayward before him, he was a teacher, but also a psychologist and mentor – challenging his athletes to become Men of Oregon.

In 1979, Jeff Nelson signed with Oregon. He may have been the most naturally gifted runner to ever run under Dellinger, except for Prefontaine. I read recently that Nelson said he didn't succeed at Oregon because Dellinger wasn't patient with him and worked him too hard when he was hurt. I cannot believe this is true. Dellinger was always cautious. I really think Jeff Nelson struggled at Oregon because he couldn't handle the freedom. He was a nice kid, and went on to achieve some great things, but the Oregon way wasn't for everybody.

I always told people, "Bill would give you enough rope to hang yourself," as a way to test whether you were mature enough to run for Oregon. Not everyone was. Like Bowerman, Bill was more interested in the eager than the talented. You had to be committed if you wanted to succeed under Bill. Under his program, you got a single sheet of paper taped on your locker every Monday with your week's workouts. You only saw him three times a week, for Tuesday, Thursday and Saturday workouts. All other runs were your responsibility. There was nobody looking over your shoulder to see if you ran. Some people made it, a lot of guys didn't—washing out because they didn't have the discipline to manage their own training.

Bill required that all his athletes take responsibility for their own lives. At 19, he was just what I needed, and 40 plus years later, that connection is still one of the most important in my life. What else can I say, except to say that I love the guy.

CHAPTER EIGHT: PRE

At Bill's encouragement, I would often train together with Pre, who had graduated the winter before and was racing in a lot of the same open meets I was. Because Pre's Oregon career had spanned both eras, I asked him which of the Bills— Bowerman or Dellinger—he preferred. He thought for a moment and then answered, "I go to Dellinger for my workouts. I go to Bowerman whenever I need my head tuned."

Maybe so, but Pre and Dellinger clearly had a special bond. When Pre was around, they were both happy. They were like brothers. Theirs was like no coach-athlete relationship I'd ever seen. I don't know if it's because they were both from rural Oregon cities, from working class families, or if it was that they both shared world class running talent, or if it was all of those things mixed together, but I know they had a bond. I hoped one day I could be even half as close to Dellinger as Pre was to him.

A lot of runners from Oregon have Pre stories, and I can't claim to have been particularly close to him. But I can claim to have pissed him off more than most.

That first fall I was at Oregon I got to know Mark Feig and Steve Bence, who were a couple of Pre's best friends. They called me up and asked me to run in this Eugene-to-Corvallis relay that would end at the Oregon State football stadium at halftime of the annual Oregon-Oregon State game (known in Oregon as The Civil War). The rivalry was huge, and this kind of long-distance massive relay was pretty new. 48 miles, with 48 different runners (students, alum, boosters, whoever) each running a single mile. The whole thing was done as a benefit for a muscular dystrophy charity.

Most of the runners were naturally going to be walk-ons or just reasonably in-shape students. But Feig and Bence's plan was to stack the last few legs of the race with the best distance runners we had, culminating in me running the 2nd-to-last mile and Pre running the final mile. At least, that was the plan. So of course I said yes. But then they asked me: can you call up Pre and ask him for us?

"Wait a sec," I said, "You're his friends. Why don't you ask him?"

"We did," Steve answered, "he said no."

112

"Well why do you think I'll get him to do any different?"

Mark grinned and said, "I just think you can."

These guys are seniors, I'm the new guy desperate for approval. How am I going to say no?

So, with these two seniors hanging over my shoulder I'm calling Prefontaine's phone number. I'm getting nervous, because you don't just dial up the god. To a freshman, this is terrifying business, but because I was from New York, I acted cool, like it didn't bother me.

He picks up.

"Yeah, what is it?"

"Pre, hey, this is Centrowitz."

"Okay..."

"Hey, we're running this, uh, 50 mile relay from Eugene to Corvallis. For muscular dystrophy—"

He cut me off. "Yeah I know."

"So, we'd like you to run."

"No."

I'm nervous as shit. What, I'm supposed to argue with Pre? "Uh... It'll be really cool... We're gonna get the lead. I'm running next to last. Hand it off to you with a 6 or 7 second lead. You'll win."

"I don't want to run. I told those guys."

He clearly doesn't. But I'm still feeling pressure from these two seniors leaning over me, trying to listen in. So, I give it one last shot.

"Pre, I promise you. I promise you I'll give you a big lead. You'll come in at halftime to the Civil War." Then, I think quickly and throw in the clincher, "And 40,000 fans will be there going crazy and screaming your name."

He thinks for a second. A long second. And then finally answers: "Okay, I'll run."

So, flash forward a few days later I'm standing there in the cold, two miles from the stadium, and around the bend down the road I see a runner coming. But it's the Oregon State runner. I count seconds until I see Feig come around the same bend. 1... 2... 3...

The Oregon State runner standing next to me was getting more and more confident and I was getting more and more nervous.

7... 8... 9...

114

Where the hell was he?

12… 13… 14…

Finally, a full 15 seconds behind comes Feig, sprinting the last hundred yards. The Oregon State guy is long gone when I get the baton. I somehow have to make up 15 seconds or show Pre I'm a liar.

I've run for a lot of things. School pride, patriotism, personal redemption, love. But that day I was running for one thing only: to avoid pissing off Pre.

I was a 4:02 miler but that Oregon State runner was no frat boy. I pulled to within 10 seconds of him. I see Pre, and within maybe 50 yards I can see he is livid. Like there's steam coming off of him. I hand him the baton and he gives me the dirtiest look I've ever seen in my life.

I hop in the team van, and everyone is cheering Pre on, but he continues to have this enormous scowl on his face. Another freshman asks out loud, "Why is Pre so mad?" I had my head down, humiliated.

Through a stroke of fortune, the first half of the football game has gone a little longer than expected and they're not quite at halftime yet. So, they hold the runners at the entrance to the tunnel that leads into the stadium. Pre is behind by 5 seconds, with just 300 meters to go. He catches his breath and paces like a tiger about to kill some poor defenseless animal. But he's up against Rich Kimball, Oregon State's best runner, who is also a 4:02 miler.

Finally the whistle blows for halftime, the fields clear, and we get word that we're good to restart the race. The official tells Pre to go on his count of five. He sends Kimball off and starts counting. 1... 2... 3...

And then Pre just goes at 3, doesn't wait until 5. I'm shocked. But who's going to say anything about it? He's Pre.

We run into the stadium and watch as Pre quickly catches up to Kimball. By the last 200 meters he's on his shoulder. The final straightaway they're stride for stride. The stadium is going nuts; the place is absolutely electric. Pre was in his element.

Rich dives at the line as Pre does his "Munich lean." I'm so far away I can't see who wins, and people swarm the finish line. Suddenly I see Pre raised up on people's shoulders. The other runners and I are ecstatic. We run over to join him and Pre shoots me the meanest look any winner of a race has ever shot. I was so scared I actually ran back to the other side of the track.

Oregon State ended up winning the game, but Oregon fans could go home with their heads held high because of Pre.

Everyone except me. His anger wasn't just Pre being a prima donna though. Like all great athletes he was deeply competitive. But he also had an enormous amount of pride. He was not going to lose to Oregon State. Losing would have been personally embarrassing, but he also would have been letting down the school he loved. That was the first time I witnessed up close Pre's competitive fire. He became an animal. Great athletes have that special quality when they're challenged. They transform from human to something else. That's what happened to Pre. He was not going to lose, no matter what. After witnessing Pre on that day, I made it my mission to emulate him. I wanted to care that much.

When they handed us the trophy for the race, there was no question who should take it home.

***

One thing Pre and I both had in common was that we didn't have any trouble putting away a half dozen or more beers in an evening. I knew Dellinger got on Pre's case about it, and pretty soon he got on mine as well.

I wasn't eligible to compete in NCAA events or wear the Oregon singlet, but I was free to race in open meets. My first race in the spring 1975 season I ran poorly—4:05 in the mile, almost two years after I hit 4:02 as a high school senior. Bill calls me into his office afterwards and says to me. "I hear from others that you're drinking too much."

I didn't know what he meant by "too much." I wasn't hungover for my races or anything. "Well," I answered, "I don't think that's the case."

Bill said, "I'll tell you what: why not, once per week, have three beers. That's it. When I was training for my last Olympics, when I won Bronze in '64, I told myself I could have one beer before dinner, one with, and one after. That was it. I stayed committed to that. I think the results speak for themselves."

I knew I was going to miss it, but if it helped me win—and helped me gain Bill's trust—I was game. We shook hands and agreed to it. Afterwards I told my friends that I had made Bill that promise and to not ever let me have more than three.

Two weeks later he took me down to the California Relays—a big time meet with lots of tradition. I was absolutely dying for some beer, but obviously didn't say anything to Bill. Before we left he gave me Peter Snell's book, *No Bugles, No Drums*. Peter Snell had matched his own world record at this meet in 1963. He ran 3:54 and closed the last 220 yards in 24 seconds. I read the book as fast as I can, thinking about how crazy that closing interval was.

118

I've been ineligible for so long that none of the other runners—all west coast guys—know who I am. I'm the furthest thing from a threat imaginable. Even my own teammates only know me by my lackluster 4:05. Instead everyone's eyes are on last year's NCAA champion in the 1500m, Paul Cummings.

The race goes out slow—almost never good for me, with my strength but more or less average closing speed. I hear the split after the first 400: 63 seconds. "Oh well," I thought, "No sub-four for me today." I tell myself to just race tough and compete.

Cummings sat at the back of the pack the whole time, close to last place. He was a kicker and could afford to do that. And at the start of the final lap, he kicks, whipping around the whole field, and we start really flying. I do everything I can to hang with him and the other leaders. With 220 yards to go I saw 3:30 on the clock. I flash back to the Snell book, remembering he ran his final 220 in 24 seconds. To break 4 minutes all I need to do is come in under 30 seconds. Of course I can do that, right? Because of the training, because of the callousing, because of that fire burning just a little bit harder than ever before, I dug even deeper.

I crossed the finish line in 4th place in 3:59.3.

Back in my hotel room after the race, I get a knock on my door. In walks Bill Dellinger, holding a six-pack. He sits down on my bed and cracks open two beers. We toast to my first sub-four minute mile and drink beer together. He's beaming. We didn't talk much—what was there to say? After about five minutes he says, 'I'm proud of you. The other four are for you. See you later." And then he walks out.

I didn't even touch the beer that night (though I more than made up for it later). More than anything, I wanted to remember that feeling. It's a choice I'm glad I made.

***

That race put some swagger in my step the rest of that spring. At long last, I'm a sub-4 man. The 78th American to break that barrier, and the 12th Oregon runner. The whole year I was this red-shirt project of Bill's, this goofy guy from the Bronx with a mustache. But now I was somebody. I had status.

On May 29, I was leaving Dellinger's office after discussing my morning run, and I bumped into Pre. We were racing in a twilight meet that night and he said, "Hey, I'm gonna run some errands today. Go to a school. Meet the Daisy Ducks

(The Daisy Ducks are an organization of women, mostly older, who support the University of Oregon sports teams – also known to bring flasks to events and knock a few down).

"You got class or you wanna come with me?"

Of course I had class. It was a Thursday. But a choice between class or hanging out with Pre?

"Nah, I got no class."

I jump in his car with him. He had a brand new, orange MGB Roadster convertible. A speedy British sports car from an era when everything British was still the height of cool. Pre owned a van and a station wagon as well, but this was his signature ride. You could spot him anywhere in Eugene when this orange Roadster came into view. And here I was riding with him in it.

Nothing we did that day was itself that glamorous. Signing autographs at a local grammar school. Meeting with the Daisy Ducks. But for the first time he was treating me, if not like an equal—because who could be—but as just another guy, someone he liked and respected. I was never star-struck by him, but I always held him in awe. And feeling like his peer for the first time was an incredible feeling.

Later in the afternoon, we stopped by his house and played cards for a few hours before the meet. Like a lot of athletes,

Pre could get edgy before a meet and cards were a good way to steady the nerves. Feig and Bence were there and somebody remembered that we were supposed to return the trophy from the Eugene-to-Corvallis race soon, so we decided to take a picture with it. The four of us lined up in front of Pre's house with the trophy while a friend took a photo with Pre's camera.

Somebody asked, "Pre, you win so many races. You even remember this one?"

He grabbed the back of my neck, hard—you can see me smiling through a grimace in the photo—and said "Yeah, I remember this race alright."

It's the only photo I ever took with Pre. Eight hours later he was dead.

***

That night was an NCAA prep meet with Oregon runners competing against a group of runners from Finland that Pre had invited over to the U.S. Like always, Pre won the 5000m in dramatic fashion, beating Olympic champion, Frank Shorter, and just missing his own American record by two seconds.

The rest of the night was pretty typical. Drinks at a local bar called The Paddock. A house party with the Finns and some other runners and coaches at Geoff Hollister's house. I honestly can't remember when I saw Pre last at the party—like a typical college guy, I was more focused on the girls.

But early the next morning I was awoken by Dave Taylor banging on my front door. I was living with Terry Williams, and we shared a phone with the unit next door, which was Dave Taylor's. Dave had gotten a call: Pre had been killed the night before in a single-car accident. He swerved to avoid an incoming car and rolled his orange MG. He ended up pinned under his car. It suffocated him. The star of American track, the hero of Eugene and one of the greatest athletes of my generation (and the guy I'd been lucky enough to spend most of the previous day hanging out with) was gone.

The next day we had our regular Saturday workout scheduled, but Bill made it known that it wasn't mandatory. Regardless, everybody showed up. But it was far from the typical practice. Dellinger handed out the workouts, but then guys just huddled in small groups, some talking to Bill, some just among themselves. They all came in their workout gear, but the practice had become a wake. Nobody wanted to run. Nobody, that is, but me.

I hope nobody found it disrespectful. We all deal with grief in our own way. Pre wasn't close to many people, and I certainly couldn't claim to be one of them. I liked him, I admired him, and I wanted to be like him. And I sure as hell felt sick he died like that. But the way I felt was that Pre would sure as hell have worked out if I died. Getting back out on the track would have been Pre's way—the Oregon way. At least my interpretation of it. So I ran.

If Bowerman handing the reigns over to Dellinger was a changing of the guard, Pre's death felt like the end of an era. The team, the school, the whole town really, felt like it was at half-mast for months after that—even through the Olympic trials the next year. He was such a transcendent talent—a native Oregonian—and a star personality. He was a celebrity, bigger than life. The vacuum he left was huge. At meets for years afterwards, the 3000m and the 5000m would always be met with more murmuring than excitement. "What would Pre's time have been?" "Pre would have left this guy in his dust." "Pre would have busted this early."

After his funeral in Coos Bay, Oregon, the University held a memorial for him at Hayward Field. 4,000 of us sat in silence as the scoreboard clock ticked to the 3-mile record Pre had made his personal quest, but never got a chance to beat: 12:36.2.

And then that summer, my mother had an aneurysm. I was back home in the Bronx, days away from an all-expenses-paid trip to the Pan Am Games in Mexico City. And suddenly she was in the hospital in a coma. In those days almost no one survived a brain aneurysm. The doctor told my sister and I she had a less than 1% chance of getting through this new surgery they were going to try. I had a ticket in my pocket and my mother about to go into the operating room. It didn't feel like there was anything I could do.

I flew down to Mexico City and ran, but I honestly can't even remember what my times were. I was waiting, almost hour-by-hour, for a call or telegram that my mother was dead. But somehow she made it through. Surviving a brain aneurysm was almost unheard of in those days, but she was one of the first ten Americans to receive this procedure, which is now common. Her motor skills would take a long time to recover—and after re-learning how to walk she would always be nervous going down stairs, or getting jostled in crowded places—but she got through it. Tough as always, she'd eventually go back to work and would go on to live another 39 years.

CHAPTER NINE: OLYMPIAN

My junior year of 1975-1976 was focused on one thing: the Olympic Trials in the coming spring. The rest of the team—and even Dellinger—may have been recovering from the shock of Pre's death, but I was determined to seize this opportunity. The Olympics obviously came around only once every four years. Everyone consoled Pre about his disappointing finish in 1972 because 1976 was just around the corner, right? You never knew what life might throw at you, so I was all in for this one.

My first efforts to prove myself didn't go so well. The NCAA Cross Country Championships were at Penn State that year. It was two years after the Nationals where I first met Dellinger and the Oregon team, and where I nearly made All-American as a freshman. This year it was different, as there was an overrepresentation of teams and runners from the nearby Northeast schools. Guys I ran against in high school, coaches who turned me down—or, in the case of Fred Dwyer—I turned down. This was a chance to prove I made the right choice by leaving that world behind and going to Oregon.

A chance that I completely blew. I had been up and down all fall, with some great times and some terrible ones. I was on an emotional roller coaster and not in control of myself. That day in late November, I didn't know it, but I was done before they ever fired the starting pistol. I had worked myself up way too much, but what a race like this required was calm confidence, determination and focus, not frantic energy. Everything I had learned during my first 18 months under Dellinger, I forgot at that meet. Sometimes that happens to young athletes. My nerves got the better of me.

I went out way too hard, in the top 10, with a 4:30 opening mile. Obviously, I couldn't sustain that pace, nobody could on a Cross Country course, and soon found myself falling further and further behind. Familiar faces whizzed past me. Craig Virgin, Nick Rose, Paul Cummings, and my roommate Terry Williams would all finish in the top ten. Then Dave Taylor, who I barely out-kicked two years earlier passed me. Then people I didn't know. Sophomores and freshman. More and more. It was getting embarrassing, but by the 4th mile I was just gassed. When people talk about the loneliness of the long distance runner, trust me, there is nothing lonelier than when you're dying, you know you've lost, and you still have two miles to go.

128

The absolute worst moment of the race was, when jogging up a hill at a snail's pace, this overweight photographer ran past me up the hill to get a shot. I was getting beat by middle-aged guys in suits, carrying two cameras and a bag full of equipment.

Two years earlier as a freshman without a coach I took 29th place. That day, as a stronger, fitter junior running for the Yankees of collegiate running under one of the greatest coaches of all time, I took 175th. Awful. I single-handedly scored more points—cross-country team points being negative like golf, the lowest score wins—than any entire *team* in Oregon history.

I self-destructed. I'd been beat by faster guys before, and I would again. But I vowed that day that no matter what, I'd never beat myself. I had gotten faster, but I still hadn't gotten mentally tougher. That was the next step.

To his credit, Bill realized he didn't need to say anything. All he offered was, "Matt, I know you're better than this." 175th place said it all.

And I knew that he was right, I was better than this. I looked at the top times and realized how I screwed myself. I could have run 5-minute pace for the first three miles and then started running negative splits. I'm sure I wouldn't have finished in the top ten, but I would have at least helped my team. Bill didn't make me feel bad about it. In fact, he rarely beat anyone up over competing poorly. His look was enough to get you to look within yourself. He didn't scold me. He was smart enough to move aside, say nothing, and let me look into a mirror and see a reflection of a guy who had beat himself. Great coaches can do that.

****

That winter, everything was about the Olympic Trials. The 1500m, an event no American had won at the Olympics since 1908, was my sole focus. Every day, every run. Bill gave each of us a goal sheet. Mine was a 3:54 mile pace—or a 3:36.7 at 1500m. My previous best 1500 was 3:41. Even Pre's best 1500 was 3:38.

The steady drumbeat of preparing for the Trials affected the chemistry of the team. We had two milers on the team that were non-Americans: Peter Spir from Canada and Randall Markey from New Zealand. Spir had also run a 3:41, and Markey a 3:39. These guys were my teammates—and at Oregon meets I'd root for them—but frankly we didn't like each other. Their loyalty was to their countries, as it should have been, and mine was to my country. However, what set me off the most about them was how dismissive they were of

Dellinger. They'd run his workouts sometimes, but other times do their own work at the direction of their national coaches. I wanted to beat the shit out of them, not just for personal and patriotic reasons, but to prove Dellinger's system was the best.

I knew I had run a 3:41 the year before, when I was mentally weaker, and had missed plenty of days from being sick or injured, so I was convinced I could get my times down. I looked at the previous year's running log. If I put 6-7 miles every day where there's a zero, and a 10 where there's a 6, and a 12 where there's a 10, I'm gonna be a hell of a lot better than last year. Better than anyone expects.

Track and Field News did a poll of American sportswriters on their picks of who would make the team. Out of the dozens surveyed only one mentioned me—as a "dark horse." Other than that, my name never appeared. I actually liked that. There was no pressure. Nobody would see me coming. I knew that I was better than everyone thought I was, and with Bill's guidance was going to run better than I'd have run before.

Dellinger's workouts were brilliant in that they were preparing me not just for a single race but for the entire three days of heats that the Trials would take. For the first time ever—or since—all three days of the 1500m heats would happen back-to-back-to-back. No off days. Which was a huge benefit to me. There were guys with more leg speed than me, but damn few stronger than me. I knew I'd be at my peak on the third day while a lot of the other guys would be feeling the weight of the heats and semis. And with each race that winter and spring I got just a little better.

And then there was the setting. For the second time in a row, the Trials would be held in Eugene at Hayward Field. I wouldn't have to deal with the discomforts of travel—and the potential of getting sick. I'd know the track. And of course the stands would be full of thousands of crazed Oregon fans, dying to see one of theirs make the Olympic Team. To avoid the many distractions accompanying the Trials, Bill had me ensconced away from the city in an A Frame house in the woods belonging to one of his close friends. I spent the days and nights leading up to the first two qualifying rounds playing cards, throwing darts and shooting pool with my best friend, "The Colonel." It was an idyllic setting with the wilderness surrounding the house providing the buffer I needed from the din and pressure of the competition as the other events were underway. After two comfortable preliminary races, I was focused and confident for the finals.

So, when I made the finals, I was confident.

The race went out at a ridiculous pace. Tom Byers, who was known for taking races out at a crazy pace, led the first 400m in a blistering 52 seconds. I kept myself composed and let him take a huge lead on the field—my first split was 55, which was also too fast. By the end of the first 800, we had reeled Byers in and I took over the lead, with a split of 1:52. I slowed the pace down a little that third lap—Bill had instructed me to save something for the final straightaway, but nobody passed me until well after the 1200 split (2:52) when Michael Durkin blew past me. Shortly after him came 800m world-record holder Rick Wolhuter, passing me around the final turn. But I didn't feel anyone else—hey, I thought, if I can stay right here, I make the Olympic team. But then I realized: I wasn't actually tired.

So, I started my kick and sprinted to the finish. There's no better feeling than when you're in a race and you still feel like you've got a lot left in the tank. As we went into the homestretch, I felt strong and even more confident that I was going to make the team. In the last ten yards I caught Durkin and took 2nd. My goal time was 3.36.7 and I crossed the finish line with a 3.36.73. I think Dellinger knew what he was doing.

I had made the Olympic team. At 21. It was a surreal feeling. My feet didn't hit the ground for days. The stands were roaring. Sure, the country would root for all of us Americans in Montreal, but right now these cheers were for me. An Oregon man. A guy they'd seen both succeed and struggle over the last two years. And I was going to represent the USA at the

Montreal Olympics. It was unreal. The dude from the Bronx was going to the Olympics.

Sure as hell better than 175th.

***

A few weeks later I found myself in Plattsburg, New York with the rest of the US Olympic Team. Training all day and then hanging out with my idols like 1972 marathon gold medalist and world-record holder Frank Shorter, Rick Wohlhuter, and Munich Olympic 4th place finisher, Don Kardong.

I was a huge Frank Shorter fan. I admired his thinking—how he was always a step ahead of everyone else. With his classic running style, he made every American proud to be a distance runner. He had been in Eugene with us the night Pre was killed, but I didn't get to know him until now.

One day some of the other distance runners—including Frank—and I decided to go to lunch at a small café in Plattsburg. I find myself at a table with seven of the best runners our country has ever produced—guys I had been reading about for years. The waitress comes over and has a funny look on her face. "Who are you fellas? Do I know you from somewhere?"

134

Frank smiles. "Sorry to disappoint you. Just some guys having lunch."

I laughed inside. Just a gold medal winner and seven of the fastest guys on earth. But I admired the way the experienced guys shrugged off the attention. They were not just champion athletes; they were champion people. How they carried themselves mattered.

By contrast, I found myself rooming with an incredibly media-savvy decathlete named Bruce Jenner. Bruce had already experienced plenty of success—with a gold at the Pan Am Games the year before, and a first place at the Olympic Trials—but he was not yet the Wheaties box Bruce, the household name. I was part of the track & field world and I only kind of knew him. But he already had an agent, and was talking about "branding" himself, concepts that I could barely understand. He knew that the media was going to focus on him prior to the games, so he was already prepared to present himself as the All American guy – the great athlete with model looks, the athlete with a beautiful blonde wife who had sacrificed everything for his Olympic dream. He had the perfect dog with him, posing for all those pre-Olympic photos. He even had all these little American flags he gave out, like he was the only one on the team representing our country. It was like he was starting a business. Nobody got rich doing track—even Pre only did okay. So, I scratched my head watching Bruce work the angles. Shows what I knew.

Years later, I saw him at the airport. We were at the gate, waiting to board the same flight. By that time, he was already a big star, having capitalized on his Olympic gold medal, the Superstar competitions, and all the other television appearances. I didn't feel confident about going up to him and introducing myself. Hell, I wondered whether he would even remember me. However, after he boarded with the other first class passengers, I boarded after him. Upon seeing him, I stopped to say hello. He looked at me and said, "Wow, Matt, what happened to you," sizing up all the added weight and my bald head. I just looked at him, without thinking, and said, "what about you, with that plastic face and everything." I look back now and think maybe I should have been more kind. I had no idea at the time, but as we now know, he was dealing with bigger issues.

When we arrived in Montreal I tried not to get overwhelmed by the moment. The kind of attention you get at the Olympics is unlike anything else in the world. And then there are all the thousands of athletes from other countries—many of them gorgeous young women—who were all around you. They gave us these national pins that we'd exchange with other athletes.

They were a great conversation starter, especially when you didn't speak each other's languages.

One day I was walking through the Olympic Village and stumbled across an unannounced small concert by Mick Jagger. He was just playing on a small stage—with a band behind him that I don't think were the rest of the Rolling Stones. Some of the female athletes were throwing their warmup tops onto the stage for him. And surprisingly, he was throwing them back. After he finished a song he said, "You don't need to do that. I came here to honor you. You're the best in the world. You don't need to honor me." And I thought: he's right, we are that cool. I admired him for that.

The other thing that I remember is what a remarkable athlete Mick was himself. At one point he was leaning back, legs folded on the ground, with the microphone in both his hands, and he raised himself up into a standing position without using his hands. It was impressive as hell. I learned later Mick's father was a gymnastics coach and one of the leading voices on physical fitness in the UK—and he designed workouts for Mick when he went on tour. I wasn't a big music guy, but I became a lifelong fan after that.

***

My goal was to make the finals. A medal would be a dream, sure, but I just wanted to be one of those top 12 guys. I knew, like in the Trials, I'll be stronger on the third day than I am on the first. I'd been nursing an Achilles injury for the last couple months, but didn't feel like it was going to be a hindrance.

But my heat went out slow, which was a bad sign for me. A typical strategy for me was to drag a fast pace and drop people, but this time I got boxed in and couldn't make a move to the front. And then at the end, when I needed a big kick, my legs just didn't have it. I finished sixth with a 3:45.02. The winner of the heat ran less than a second ahead of me—3:44.18. But that was all the difference – lesson learned about heats at the Olympics. You better be ready to run when the real race starts, often more than half way through the event, and if you're not ready, you'll be watching from the stands, which is exactly what I would do.

Frankly, I was humiliated. I let Bill down, my country down, and myself. I was feeling pretty bad, but I took solace in the fact that nobody from New York had even come to watch me compete. It's not that they didn't care, it's just that although NYC was just six hours from Montreal, it would have been an expensive trip for people from the Bronx – they had to work, so nobody came. Like I said, I was feeling down. Bill put so much work into me, leading up to this disappointing finish. I was tempted to leave then and there but he persuaded me to stick around and watch the finals. It was a hard pill to swallow but I took it.

I'm glad I did, because it was eye-opening. My jaw literally dropped. Even if I had made the finals, I realize that day that there was no way I could ever medal in the 1500. John Walker won with a final lap of 52 seconds. I didn't have that kind of leg speed—you're either born with it or you're not. When you see the 'real deal' guys run you can't fool yourself.

I knew right then that to be a true global contender I'd have to move up in event distance. So, I watched the 5000m final. They came in with great times of course, Lasse Virén winning in 13:24.76, but I broke it down: basically, a 9-minute two mile and then a 4:05 mile. I could do that. Not right now, but if I trained hard enough for the next four years, I could get there. So, that day I became a 5000m man.

Dellinger said, "Alright. But you've got to train like a 5000 meter guy. And keep running the 1500 and miles." And I agreed. But sitting there in Montreal, watching guys I trained with make their finals and take medals, Moscow in 1980 felt like a lifetime away.

***

I left Montreal early, riding back to New York City with a friend of mine who was a cop. We got pulled over on the way down—he didn't get a ticket of course—by the same cop he got pulled over on the drive up. Crazy.

I partied hard that summer in New York, and carried over that energy when I came back to Eugene in the fall. I wasn't burned out—I still wanted to run—but it's hard to get excited about beating Washington State when you've just been to the Olympics. I found I had a new priority: enjoying college life.

Instead of focusing exclusively on running and associating with other runners, I realized what being a big athlete on campus could do for you, especially in Eugene if you were a track star. I learned how to walk into parties and take control. I schmoozed professors, hung out with the dean. I had women throwing themselves at me.

I still felt an obligation to not let down my teammates. No matter how late I partied I made it to practice every morning. But that hunger to run for myself was pretty low at that point. In '76, I was consumed by my running, but honestly in '77 and '78 I just wasn't.

After the previous year, where we were all shaking off the shock of Pre's death, a number of gifted young runners—

Alberto Salazar from Massachusetts, Rudy Chapa from Indiana, Don Clary from Alaska, and Eugene's own Billy McChesney—all brought new energy and excitement to Hayward Field. I saw the promise in these guys, and I tried to mentor them, but my heart wasn't quite into it. I guess I had the post-Olympic blues. The one good thing about my senior year was that after my horrible performance in the NCCAA Cross Country Championships the prior year, we won this time. Like Pre, I was now also part of a national championship team.

In 1977, I was technically a senior, but I successfully petitioned for a fifth year. Since I redshirted a year and changed my major from Manhattan it was approved. So, I got a new lease on college life for another year, but I could feel the end was looming. I was starting to realize I wasn't going to be a kid forever.

That last year I won some races and lost some, but I wasn't concerned with my win-loss record. It was all about putting in the miles, putting 'money in the bank' that I'd be able to cash out in 1980: or at least that's what I thought at the time. The whole time Bill was helping me develop workouts, building me into a stronger and stronger 5000m runner. I was mostly racing in the mile—with decent but unexceptional times. My best that year was a 3:39.6 at the NCAA Championships, with a bad last 200 that gave me a 6th place finish.

Just before I graduated in the spring of 1978, I was forced to make a decision that would test my relationship with my mentor. Nike was putting together a new post-collegiate track program, called Athletics West (AW). Athletics West was creating a revolutionary post-graduate training program to support athletes who wanted to continue training and offered me a $12,000 annual salary. On top of that they'd provide free housing, a company car, travel expenses, massage, doctor expenses, and health insurance. A deal like this is pretty standard for elite athletes today but was unheard of in 1978.

I'd be one of just twelve athletes in the program and felt very honored they wanted me to be a part of it. Their first signed runner was none other than Craig Virgin. But there was a catch: even though I would still be living in Eugene, I wouldn't be permitted to keep training with Bill. The Athletics West coach was none other than Harry Johnson, who in many ways was Dellinger's nemesis. Harry had been a hugely successful high school coach at South Eugene high school, and there were a lot of track fans in Eugene that wanted to see Harry replace Bill at the University of Oregon. With just two years until the Olympics, and my deep emotional bond with Bill, I couldn't see any way I was going to be able to run for A.W. I was in a painful position.

I was 22 years old, from a poor family, and had never made more than a few bucks an hour. My mother by this point had recovered to the point she was working again as a full-time maid in New York, but she was making less than $10,000 a year. So, to me this deal was incredible. Nike was an exciting new runner's company with deep roots in Oregon track, and the long-term professional associations were really appealing. Nike was far from the massive global brand it is today, but it was exploding in the running world and its future looked very bright.

At the time I found it very difficult to understand why Athletics West would put me in this position, why they would insist I walk away from my coach. I knew there had been tension between Dellinger and Bowerman, which also meant tension between Dellinger and Nike, particularly as it related to the Oregon track team, but I didn't realize how deep that rivalry had developed by this point.

I immediately told Dellinger about the offer. He didn't react emotionally, just asked what I wanted to do. I told him in an ideal world I would join A.W. and still be coached by him. "Well, we don't live in that world, do we?" he responded.

I took a week to make my decision. I finally came back to Bill and told him that it was more important to train under him than to have all the luxuries of Athletics West. Even though I honestly had no idea how I was going to support myself while putting in the long hours needed to train for the Olympics, I knew that Bill had gotten me this far, so I was going to stick with him. Plus, I loved the guy like a father. I needed him.

Dellinger and I didn't agree on everything. We both have strong personalities, and by this time I knew my body better than anyone—I demanded a say in my workouts and strategy. But by this point we had developed a unique relationship. I had run through a series of father figures throughout my early life, but in Bill I felt I had finally found a real father. I loved the guy and trusted him more than anyone. I knew I wasn't going to run under him forever, but I wasn't going to risk everything I'd built so far in my preparation the 1980 Games by switching to an unknown coach.

Bill thanked me and then told me to come back to his office the next day—didn't say another word. So, 24 hours later I walk back in and he announces he's lined up an opportunity with a local Oregon shoe company called OSAGA. OSAGA had a modest presence in Eugene at the time—they sponsored the scoreboard at Hayward Field for a while—and were sold in mom and pop shoe stores around the state. They saw the success Nike was having after their breakout moment at the '76 Olympics and were looking to expand. OSAGA had yet to endorse any athletes or coaches, and Bill, unbeknownst to me, had worked out a deal with their vice-president of promotion that would allow me to train and race full time.

So, a few days later I met with the vice-president of promotion, getting a full tour of their headquarters in Eugene. The guy asked me what I thought an appropriate salary would be. I stammered. Somehow I had assumed Bill worked that out beforehand. But suddenly in walks the owner of the company, Bill Combs. Bill was already very successful in real-estate and owned several of the high end boutique stores in Oregon. He saw that this negotiation wasn't going anywhere, so he made it simple for me: "What is Athletics West offering you?"

I didn't know a thing about negotiating, so I thought, might as well answer honestly: "Twelve thousand dollars."

"Okay," he said, without a moment's hesitation, "We'll pay you 14."

And that was it. My jaw dropped. I was expecting to be offered much less. When they came in well over A.W.'s offer I immediately became loyal and gung-ho to Bill Combs and OSAGA—and even stronger in my commitment to Bill Dellinger.

I had weathered a lackluster two years after the Olympics, but after my OSAGA deal I felt reborn. From that point on, for the next two years that I ran for OSAGA, I never lost a single race at Hayward Field or the U.S. Nationals to an Athletics West runner. I would rather have cut off my leg than lose to AW. That's what loyalty does. It's not that I had a personal animosity towards Nike or any of the Athletics West guys, but my objective was to show my loyalty to my coach. The belief Dellinger and Combs showed in me that year forged a life-long bond between us.

When I graduated, Bill gave me a simple card. It said "I look forward to continuing our friendship." Long after that day I would continue to refer to Bill as my coach, but realizing he considered me a friend was one of the most powerful moments of my life. I treasure that card—and our enduring friendship—to this day.

CHAPTER TEN: END OF THE LINE

The rumblings over a boycott started late in 1979 but I did everything I could to ignore them. When I did think about it, I convinced myself it couldn't happen. Somebody would realize how stupid this is. America doesn't boycott. We don't avoid our enemies on the field of competition—we beat them. Politics and sports had always been separate, and of all the international turmoil I'd seen in my short life, I really couldn't understand why this year was any different.

I was rounding into great form for the 5000m in the Trials. I had taken gold in the 1979 Pan Am Games in Puerto Rico, with a 14:01 in unbelievable humidity. I was stronger than I'd ever been, and mentally tougher. I can never be that guy who claims I would have won this or that—there are too many variables in winning at that elite level—until you prove it, you haven't won anything. But I knew that if 1976 was a learning experience, this was going to be my real opportunity to show what I was made of.

And then in May, just a month before the Olympic Trials, President Carter announced we'd be boycotting the Olympics. 66 other countries followed our lead—including China, West Germany, and Japan. And that was it. In the best shape of my life, faced with the opportunity of my lifetime, it was just not going to happen. No Olympics.

Some guys didn't even bother to show up at the Trials. I figured, it's a track meet. It's the event I've trained for. I have to at least follow through. Again, on my home track of Hayward Field—and in front of screaming Oregon fans who did everything they could to make this race feel like the most important one in the world—I opened up with a punishing pace and held on through the finish line, winning first place in a time of 13:30.62. The mood was obviously different from the previous Olympic Trials—nobody kidded themselves that this meant nearly the same thing—but beating every other guy in America in your event still felt pretty good.

About a month after the Olympic Trials, they invited us to Washington D.C. for a special event and awarded us honorary medals. When I got back to my hotel room, I looked at myself in the mirror with the "Gold Medal" and thought, I did everything I could. That evening Alberto Salazar—who got a "Bronze"—and a few other guys from Oregon dragged me out to an evening event they were also throwing for the

Olympians. I didn't feel like celebrating, but I didn't want to let the guys down. We were all still wearing our medals and trying to feel good about ourselves. When we got to a discotheque, outside of the dance hall, I see Larry Stanaford, the trainer at the University of Oregon, my god, he's wearing a gold medal, identical to mine. I think, "That's weird, who let Larry walk around with their medal?" Then we get into the club and I'm shocked to see dozens of people—far more than there are events in the Trials—wearing "Gold" medals. Clearly the Trials folks had ordered hundreds of these honorary medals and at some point just started giving them away as cheap mementos. So suddenly my special honor felt not so special.

I couldn't deal with it, so I went back to my room and passed out at 8 or 9 o'clock. I was so down I fell asleep with all my clothes on, even my cowboy boots. Picture it. A dude from the Bronx, dead asleep from total disappointment, wearing cowboy boots. All this without a single drop of booze. I woke up the next morning wondering if any of it even happened.

In the lobby, I saw a newspaper: The Washington Post. On the front page they had a picture of the Olympic athletes wearing their medals. Everyone else looks distracted, but dead in the center is me, standing proudly at attention, wearing my gold medal.

***

Training yet another four years for 1984 felt beyond comprehension at that point. So I decided my life needed a big change, and I moved back to New York City. I was twenty-five years old, and had no idea what the future had in store for me.

I kept up my training and racing, staying in constant long-distance contact with Dellinger. He was no longer formally coaching me but offered guidance on my workouts, and I offered some insights into the occasional headstrong young runner he had trouble corralling.

I took a job as an assistant track coach at St. Johns University, under head coach Duffy Mahoney, and lived with a young married couple in Queens. I immediately knew that I loved connecting with young runners—especially those from underprivileged backgrounds like mine—but my heart wasn't fully into coaching yet. Not at 25 in New York City, with all the distractions that were available to me.

My 5000m times kept getting better, and I won the USA Outdoor Championships four years in a row—from 1979 to 1982. And in 1982 ran probably the greatest race of my life in the Prefontaine Classic.

The Pre Classic—once the "Bowerman Classic" until renamed after Pre's untimely death—had become one of the premiere meets in the world. Held annually at Hayward Field in June, it drew some of the best athletes from all over the world. American 5000 meter times had been coming down fast in the last few years. I had won here in 1979 with a 13:40, and then in 1981 with a 13:27. But recently Marty Liquori had set a new American record with a 13:15.

The word got out that both Alberto Salazar—now graduated from Oregon and running for Athletics West—and I were going to make a run at Liquori's record. The always engaged Hayward Field crowd was even more electric that day, as two of their favorite sons were preparing to battle head to head for the record.

Alberto was by then the superior longer distance runner, one of the best and most versatile long distance runners in the world. Just two months earlier he had out-dueled Dick Beardsley to win the 1982 Boston Marathon in one of the all-time great finishes. Combined with his two New York City Marathon wins, he was on his way to becoming a worldwide celebrity. But though I'd never touch him in a marathon or even a 10,000m, in the 5,000 he only had a slight edge on me, and if I could hang with him until the final 800 I knew I could out-kick him.

As expected, Alberto set a very aggressive pace, taking the lead and daring us to keep up. Paul Cummings, Ralph King, and I took his dare and lined upbehind Alberto as he did everything he could to out-drag us. Over the first two miles, Paul would edge close to Alberto, letting him know we were still there, but I hung about five meters back. The savvy Oregon crowd got more and more excited as they saw the splits. We ran a blistering 4:15 opening mile, and nearly matched it with a 4:17 second mile. But Alberto still couldn't shake us.

Finally, as we entered the last 800, Alberto picked up the pace and began his long-sustained kick. He knew this was his only path to victory, as he did not possess the leg speed to outkick anyone in the field. As we approached the final 400, I surged past King and Cummings to ride Alberto's shoulder. When I was still there with the last 300 ahead, I knew I had it. On the back straightaway I kicked past Alberto and started to race the clock. If I could close fast enough, with a final 400 under 60 seconds, I could take down Liquori's record.

In that last 400, all my training, all my work with Dellinger, all my mental callousing paid off. I ran it in 57.9 and took the American record with a 13:12.91, the sixth fastest time in the world then. If I'd done it just five years earlier it would have been a world record.

I put my arm around Alberto and we ran our victory lap together as the home crowd went wild. It was a great feeling. And even though Alberto took second that day, he'd get the last laugh, breaking my record just a month later in Stockholm with a 13:11.93. At least I had it for a a few weeks.

I was 27 years old, and would never again run faster.

***

Later that year I was in Oslo for the Bislett Games, preparing to make an attempt at Henry Rono's world record of 13:06.2. I had planned to run the 3,000m to get myself up to speed for the 5000 a few days later. But the meet organizers badly wanted Norwegian runner Øyvind Dahl to win the 3000, so they paid me a little extra money "under the table" to run the mile instead. I wasn't making much as an assistant coach, and it didn't really affect my preparation, so I took it. (By the way, for any track and field fan that is under 40, you should all know that all money earned by track and field athletes back in the early 80's was paid "under the table." We were technically amateur athletes back then. If it were known you were being paid for competing, you could be banned.)

There were so many moments where Fate—or God, or whatever you want to believe it is—intervened to my benefit. Moving to Queens at the right time. Meeting Brother Bielen. Meeting Dellinger. Getting to know Pre. I can't complain when

Fate decides it's given me so much it's time to take back. And that day it did.

On the third lap, a runner in front of me stumbled and fell. Instinctively, I hurdled over him. I felt a twinge in my hamstring. I had suffered an Achilles injury back in '76 and various minor ailments over the years, but I'd never had a problem with my hamstring. This felt strange but the pain wasn't excruciating so I kept running on it. I didn't realize it then but I'd torn it, and by running the rest of that race I continued to tear it worse and worse. I ran 3:54 for that mile, my best ever. And I didn't even go all out—knowing I had the 5000 around the corner. But that was it. I tore it and was never the same. And instead of me breaking the world record two days later, it was Dave Moorcroft, who scorched Henry Rono's world record by an unreal 5.79 seconds and running what at that time was an ungodly 13:00.41.

Fate might have taken my speed away in 1982, but it gave back when I met a friend of my roommate's teammate, Beverly Bannister, at a party. We hit it off right away, and even though my female roommate advised Beverly not to date me—because apparently I never returned the phone calls of all the girls who used to call the house—she went against her better judgment and pretty soon we fell in love. For the first time in my life, I didn't just have a steady girlfriend, I had somebody in my life I wanted to build something with, make sacrifices for. And, it turns out, she was a 2:08 half-miler in college. So, if we ever had kids, they just might have some wheels.

Throughout 1983 and 1984 I continued to train and race, nursing my hamstring and hoping a return to full fitness was just around the corner. But as the spring approached I was still running on a bum leg. I didn't even run in the Olympic Trials. This was especially painful because the Trials were for the Los Angeles Olympic Games. I watched as old friends and foes like Doug Padilla (who I had smoked in that Pre Classic in 82), Steve Lacy, and Don Clary qualified in the 5000m with 13:26, 13:27, and 13:28, times I could have easily bested pre-injury. Paul Cummings and Craig Virgin qualified in the 10,000m. Alberto in the marathon.

Instead of running in the first American-hosted Olympics since 1932, I was watching on TV like everybody else. The L.A. setting for these Games put the media coverage into overdrive. Anyone who was a star at these Games would become a huge media sensation. There aren't too many things tougher than watching a televised world sporting event take place when you feel like you should be there.

But my life was inexorably moving away from running. One evening I took Dellinger out to dinner at a restaurant called Tino's in Eugene. I'd always valued his advice—on running and on life—and finally asked him, "I think I'm going to marry Beverly. I want to know what you think."

Bill put his knife and fork down slowly and answered, "I think you're asking the wrong guy." He was right, his marriage had been a difficult one.

After weeks of building up to this conversation, this was all I could get out of him. He didn't even finish his meal—we moved onto drinking after that. In September of 1984, Beverly and I got married and began talking about the sacrifices and challenges of raising a family together.

I knew retirement was looming. It was hard to hang it up, but it became clear by the following year my body was just never going to be the same. I decided the USA Outdoor Championships in Indianapolis would be my last race. I didn't announce it to anybody—besides Dellinger and Beverly—and I honestly expected to perform poorly. Most of the field at that point were faster than me. But I got one last gift before my career ended.

It was unusually hot and Doug Padilla set a punishing pace for the first two miles. Most of the pack chased him and as the last mile started they began to hit the wall left and right. I was easily a 100 meters behind but I found myself starting to pick up dead meat. Conditioning wasn't my problem; it was my lack

156

of a kick with my weak hamstring. And in a race where I hoped just to avoid disappointment I amazingly took third, in 13:28. I couldn't have been happier.

An old friend once told me that athletes don't retire -- they get cut. Well, that might be true in well-funded professional sports, but in track and field, you have to make the long, painful and very personal decision on when to retire. Nobody ever tells you to your face that you're done. It's often that you just can't afford it, or your body stops working for you, or sometimes, you just decide it's time to do something different. Then again, maybe it's as simple as what Tom Hanks says in the movie *Forrest Gump*, when he stops running: "I'm pretty tired. I think I'll go home now." Regardless, I decided just before this last rac, that I was finished.

At 30 years old, I was retired.

CHAPTER ELEVEN: COACH

I was never concerned for my own livelihood. I had grown up with nothing, in a family and a neighborhood where having nothing was normal. So, as a former Olympian with a college degree, I wasn't too worried about myself. But I was married now, and Beverly was talking about starting a family. Supporting a wife and possibly kids? That I didn't know how to do.

Like a lot of former runners, I tried working for a shoe company. Adidas needed salesmen and I was well-known in running circles. Selling sneakers kept me connected to running—I'd attend local college meets, high school meets, offer advice when kids asked me. While I was no natural businessman, I was booking orders.

In the middle of the summer of 1988, I was down at a local track at the end of a workday. I wasn't in great shape, but trying to at least stay healthy and avoid Bill's prediction of my waistline at 40. To avoid the embarrassment of getting passed by people I was jogging the opposite way—clockwise—around the track. To my surprise I ran into Ross Donahughe, a former Villanova runner and sub-4-minute guy, who was near the tail-end of his career.

I yelled out, "Hey Ross!" but he didn't recognize me. It was dark, he was in lane 1, I was in 8, and I was fat and slow. I was starting to look like Robert De Niro when he played Jake La Motta. I'm not talking about the fit La Motta portrayed by De Niro, I'm talking the retired Jake, with the big belly. Well, I walked over to Ross and he finally made the connection. We caught up and I congratulated him for qualifying for the '88 Olympic Trials. I asked what he was doing for his workout and he said, "Well I don't know, what do you think?"

I thought, well okay, you're going to the Olympic Trials, you're warmed up, and you don't know what you're doing. A little odd. So, I asked him "Well what were you planning on doing?"

He answered, "I have a sore Achilles. But I was planning to run 8x400 starting at 54 seconds and try to hang on the best I can."

From experience I knew he could end up doing his Achilles more harm than good. So, I offered, "Tell you what, let's start at 60 and work your way down to 54. I think that might be better." He agreed and ended up having a great workout.

Afterwards Ross asked for my help laying out a workout schedule leading up to the Trials, which were about three weeks away. I was happy to help him, and we met in person and over the phone over the following few days. He started to look better and better with each workout. Going into the Trials I told him that he needed to get into the habit of winning. Everyone in the field is going to run conservative, sit back, and kick home. What I wanted him to do is run every race like it was the final. I knew Ross wasn't lightning fast, but I did know he was in shape enough to recover. Like me, he was strong, so I wasn't worried about recovery between rounds.

He ended up taking first in the first heat. Then in the semis he runs the race like I counseled him and he qualified for the finals. Suddenly the buzz was all about Ross's big comeback and his chance to make the Olympics again. He ended up only taking 9th in the Finals—he was just no longer fast enough to take on younger guys like Steve Scott—but he was genuinely happy with his performance in the Trials.

A few days later, I got a call from my old coach Frank Gagliano asking, "How in the hell did you get those performances out of Ross?" Gags was at Georgetown by then, and as luck would have it Adidas asked me to take on a senior sales job in the D.C. market. So, when I moved down Gags invited me to be a volunteer coach and run with his guys at Georgetown. It went well and he asked me to coach their cross-country team in the fall. We lost our first few meets but built up the strength of the team. By season's end, we wound up winning Georgetown's first IC4A in over 20 years.

Gags certainly deserves most of the credit, but we produced some great runners in that period, including two 1992 Olympians—John Trautman in the 5000 and Steve Holman in the 1500. Suddenly the sleepy Georgetown track team was very much in demand among talented high school runners.

But as fulfilling as helping the Georgetown runners was, it didn't pay the bills. And then Adidas decided on a different corporate strategy: they'd make more shoes but in fewer categories. Suddenly they didn't need a dedicated running shoe salesman in D.C., so I got axed. And my small family headed back to New York City.

***

My next enterprise was a dive into the coffee business. Knowing I was looking for a way to make a living, Dellinger connected me with a gourmet coffee roaster based in Oregon. They were looking for a distributor on the east coast, and if I could find a partner to put up some money, I felt I could make the sales of the coffee beans to the thousands of restaurants in New York. At the time there was no Starbucks—people pretty much drank Folgers—but I'd been over to Europe and had the Italian-style espresso and knew there was no comparison. I thought there could be a huge market for gourmet coffee in this country if only people had a chance to try it.

The first partner I connected with was a friend named Brendan who lived on Long Island. He was an amateur runner and owned a couple of bars, making pretty good money. Brendan tells me he is in, but that we need at least one more partner with access to capital.

So, my brother-in-law connects me to this Bronx big-shot named Vinny Promuto. Vinny is a natural businessman and has made a killing in the waste management business. He pioneered transporting garbage from New York all the way to Ohio where it would be compressed and dumped in local landfills. And he's an athlete, having played college football at Holy Cross and then professionally with the Washington Redskins. So, because of his reputation he's one of the few guys in the Bronx who doesn't have to pay a vig to the mob.

At the time, Vinny was building a new garbage transfer station. With my brother-in-law's introduction I headed out there in a brand new suit to meet with him in his trailer. It smells, naturally, like garbage, but I don't let it bothering me, giving

Vinny my best pitch. He says no. I come back again, still no. I come back a total of nine times, getting a rejection every single time. On the 9th visit, Vinny says "Kid, why do you keep wearing a suit. You a stockbroker or something?"

"No," I said.

"Are you wearing that suit just for me?"

I nodded.

He laughs and says, "Next time you come back here, don't wear the suit."

He made me wait two weeks for a follow-up appointment, but finally I met with him again, a tenth time, and he said yes to my proposal. So finally Brendan and I landed the biggest partner in the Bronx. And to make it even better, Vinny got us a spot at Huntspoint Market, one of the largest wholesale markets in the world. We named our company VBM Custom Roasting (for Vinny, Brendan, Matthew) and launched with enormous optimism.

I took a modest salary from the business, enough to support Beverly and our two young kids (Lauren and Matthew), and threw myself completely into the business. For the last five years I'd been at least partially connected to the track world—attending meets, counseling runners, talking to coaches—but I was totally consumed in the business. Now I hustled as hard as I ever trained for a race. I would walk up and down 1st and 2nd avenue, restaurant to restaurant. Cuban restaurants, Italian restaurants, Greek restaurants. Hard selling every manager and owner I could meet. Compared to that—when I finally returned to coaching, recruiting an athlete would never seem remotely like a challenge.

But we launched our business in 1991 and were hit hard by the early 1990s recession. Customers started to have trouble making their payments. I had the choice of cutting them off—shrinking our business—or floating them for a while. I gambled on my customers and floated them. In my desire for success, I extended too much credit. We started to spiral. And then in 1994 the first Starbucks opened in New York. And the writing was on the wall. We finally closed up shop in 1995.

For the first time in my life I cried over failure. I had never worked so hard to achieve so little. I was 40 years old and had less idea of what I was going to do next than any time since I was 15. And yes, as Dellinger predicted, I wasn't just out of shape, I was fat. And bald. I mailed him a check for $100 the day I turned 40.

***

We moved back to Washington D.C. and I took a low-paid coaching job at American University for what was basically a glorified intramural program. We weren't a real NCAA track program, but I enjoyed working with the students, who were truly passionate about running. In retrospect, it was a great, low-stakes testing ground for some of the principles and techniques of coaching I'd later use. It was a lot of trial and error. Like my running, I used things from the four great coaches of my past and blended it into my own style.

In 1996 American hired a new athletic director, Lee McElroy, and reinstated the track program, hiring me to a full-time position and giving me two scholarships. I knew I had to be patient. I wasn't going to make this a national-caliber team overnight. I kept reminding myself to stay in the present and not get ahead of myself—and certainly not promise the AD, or the boosters, or the student-athletes themselves, anything impossible. The same goes for running as it does in coaching— the only thing you can take care of is today.

Most great athletes don't make great coaches. I think this is the case because so many of them don't have the patience. Success often comes a lot easier for the world-class talents than for the average college athlete. I really think that it's because of a hyper-competitive drive that often turns coaches

166

into bullies instead of mentors. Frank Gagliano once told me, back when I was still assisting at St. John's, "You can't be a championship runner and a championship coach simultaneously." As an athlete you're hungry for results right now: you want to see immediate progress next week, next month, next quarter. As a coach and as a parent, you have to be patient.

The bread and butter of my coaching style were the five core Oregon principles handed down to me by Dellinger: Moderation, Progression, Variation, Adaptation, Callousing. I'd offer those to any new coach as a powerful foundation of any coaching style. And whatever success I've had as a coach is largely due to the wisdom I've inherited. But over the years I've also added some concept and principles of my own:

The Three H's

The biggest challenge of this job is keeping things fresh - both physically and mentally. With what I like to call The Three H's — 1) Healthy 2) Happy 3) Hungry.

The key to this paradigm is mental and physical *Health*. Without health, nothing is fun. And without consistent health, you cannot improve in this sport. Keeping athletes healthy involves a variety of training ingredients - different types of terrain, intervals, volume, and, most importantly, the ability to adapt to changes in weather or stress. Each recipe for each kid is different.

When athletes are healthy and able to enjoy their training and racing, they are happy. This allows us to cultivate a fun environment where athletes feel like they are improving. Improvement and progression builds confidence, which ultimately fuels their desire to compete. It makes them hungry for competition.

The more health an athlete enjoys during the year through a lack of sickness and uninterrupted training, the more they enjoy running. One of the best feelings an athlete can have is to feel that he or she is invincible - superior to their competitors. This stems from being healthy year-round, or enjoying uninterrupted training. Happiness also comes from the environment — take me as example, I was physically healthy during my time at Manhattan College, but I was not happy in my environment—so I stagnated as a runner.

Happiness is deeply underrated. That is why 100% of the time I give an athlete a release from our school if he or she is unhappy. Sometimes you change majors, sometimes your priorities change and another school will be a better fit — whether it is academic or money reasons. I will never begrudge an athlete for seeking an environment that makes them happy.

Miserable athletes almost never succeed—and running is too hard and life is too short to be unhappy doing it.

Even though the majority of our athletes dramatically drop their times, not everyone is naturally *Hungry* to win. That requires a different level of thinking than just running faster yea- to-year. I won 4 consecutive national titles. It was a lot more fun winning the first one than having to defend the next three. Hunger doesn't always naturally sustain. You have to stay hungry. Each year I would have to re-dedicate myself to the goal of winning another national title. In the dead of winter with all the holiday parties, it is very easy to forget how soon June and July come around. Each time I would have to re-focus and stay hungry.

Certain times you have to trick yourself into re-dedication. Running certain races that you weren't going to win because you were going in underprepared. I would get a little beat up and it would be a reminder how tough the competition really is. I would also travel to Oregon during my winter break for 10 days and train with world-class younger guys on the Oregon team like Salazar, McChesney and Clary, and the level of intensity would be much more than I was presently doing on my own. Their hunger would rub off on me.

Flexibility

You have to be flexible. But how do you become flexible when your training requires you to be rigid? You can't control the environment or the weather. You can't even count on the track being cleared or open. This is certainly more important on the east coast than the west coast. The weather patterns are much more temperate on the west coast. New York City is obviously a city of extremes. Everything is amplified. Every day is a battle. I learned very quickly that I needed to be fluid and ever changing as the cliché says: it is not written in stone. Many times I had to remind myself and I continue to remind my athletes that you have the power to change any given situation. Being stubborn is not a sign of dedication.

Find your run

At one point in college I was feeling stagnant. Physically I was fine, but mentally I was stale. I turned to Dellinger for help. I went into his office and explained how I was feeling. He began describing to me his favorite run he had ever done. When he graduated from college in the late 1950s, he joined the Coast Guard and was assigned to a radar base on an isolated part of the Washington coastline. Every day he would train on the beach. There were no lined tracks, or marked trails anywhere near him, so he was training unconventionally for the year he spent at the base.

He was sitting in his office chair, leaned back with one leg resting on the edge of his desk. He painted the scene beautifully. He was up early, the sun barely peaking over the mountains. Fog rolled in off the ocean. The whole place seemed alive, trees swaying; breathing in and out with the coastal wind. He started his run on the beach; the sand packed from high tide the night before, perfect footing. The smell of sea-salt filled his nostrils as he navigated the coast-line.

He turned left, starting the ascension into the coastal woods. Debris from the Washington pines softened the contact of his foot on the ground, making for a cushioned ride through the forest trails. He wound his way up through the woods. The trail opened up and he came across a clearing. What he saw next was astounding. His eyes widened as he is described the run. I'm on the edge of my seat. His story was so vivid, the way he talked about it made me feel like I was there. I needed to hear what was next; what it was he saw in that clearing.

Without warning, he swings his foot off the desk and bolts upright in his chair, moving towards me; his nose only about an inch from my face. I'm startled, but frozen. Quietly he says to me, "That was my run, now you have to go find yours." Soon after I would find my run in an 18-miler along the Mackenzie River outside of Eugene.

I've told this story dozens of times to my athletes through the years. It's important to have a place where you can mentally reflect and embrace in hard work.

No Days Off in Thinking

To be successful on the national and international level, you need to stay plugged into the mission. It takes a lot more energy just to live in America compared to living in a third-world country where you are isolated and the pace is slower. Life is busier, more distracting. There are so many things demanding attention and time from a college athlete. We have to learn how to pace ourselves, to manage our energy to get through the day and still complete a challenging workout at the end of it all.

It is very hard to get into a training routine or training pattern. Once you get into a pattern that is working for you, it is very important to stay there. And it's important to remember that school provides distractions but also a valuable structure. You have a team, training tables, tutors, and coaching resources at your fingertips. Once you travel home for winter break for approximately 6 weeks, you must organize most things for yourself. It is important that the athlete stays plugged in to the high school or college program wherever they travel.

That's where discipline comes in, and staying focused on your goals. There are always things trying to separate you from your goals – holiday gatherings and parties, family obligations and personal situations that can throw you off track. It is paramount that you keep open communication with your coach, your teammates, and even previous coaches you have worked with—whoever motivates you. You have to remember – there is always a championship waiting around the corner.

It is very normal to have obstacles and problems growing up in life and in track. But it is the championship thinking that will get us over those hurdles. It takes sacrifice to put aside the distractions and chase our dreams. Growing up in the Bronx, there were plenty of people who had tough family lives, tough living situations – divorce, alcohol and drug addiction, criminal backgrounds – yet they still went about their daily routine; work, paying their bills, all with a smile on their face. New York City is where I learned about championship thinking, from people who faced their problems and handled them. They didn't always succeed, but they never shied away from addressing any problem. I have yet come across anyone who is blessed with a carefree existence.

The same goes in life as it does in running – you never want to be surprised. Slow start, fast start, surge in the middle, very fast finish, you must keep training to prepare for any situation. Most runners are more comfortable running in the pack. But you must be accustomed to both leading *and* following. We force our runners to take the lead in intervals during practice so they are prepared for anything that can happen in a championship race.

Struggle

As all parents, teachers, and coaches know, hitting plateaus, slumps, and flat periods is a normal part of growing up. The student-athlete is frequently challenged with fears and doubts about the classroom, social settings, their place on the team. I believe it is a key part of our job to assist them through this process. The key word being assist – not to get ahead of them during these stages of development. Sometimes it is better for us to give them more space and time to deal with these issues and problems – to struggle with them. It is certainly not easy as a parent, coach or friend to stand by and watch anyone struggle for a solution or an answer. Especially nowadays where everything is instantaneous – it can get be discouraging to deal with the process of growing, setting and reaching goals, and sometimes just fitting in.

174

After dealing with hundreds of young people, both men and women (including my own children), there are no rules, time limits or expectations for everyone's development. There are no two kids exactly the same. It makes it difficult to guide, coach, or parent a young person through the process of growing and dealing with rejection, failure and just plain dealing with the struggle of the day-to-day routine.

Know Thyself

A running log is essential. A distance runner must keep detailed records of workouts and races, including pertinent details such as weather, running surfaces, effort given during each session, shoes work, etc. The log is an athlete's road map to success. Or at the very least, it is a written record of what went wrong and what went right. Both coach and athlete can use it to pinpoint when and where the breakthrough happened.

***

With these principles, and of course years of hard work by some very talented and motivated young athletes, our program at American University has produced 20 All-

Americans so far, more than the entire Patriot League combined. We won six straight conference championships in cross country. Our coaching staff has produced coaches over the years that have gone on to lead other high-caliber Division I programs, including Kentucky (Sean Graham), Manhattan College (Kerry Gallagher), and George Washington University (Terry Weir).

But most important, we're having fun. I don't make the most money, I don't drive the nicest car, and I don't have the biggest office. But I'm happy in my own skin. I watch a lot of coaches around the country, and too many seem like they aren't having fun. I'd rather be me than them.

CHAPTER TWELVE: FATHER

People often ask my kids—especially the two who became internationally competitive runners—what it was like growing up under Matt Centrowitz. Their answer is typically that they really didn't know I was anything special as a runner. They knew I coached and knew I had once run myself, but I made a point of never dwelling on my past accomplishments. As Brother Bielen had advised, I put all of my medals and trophies away (save for my honorary gold from 1980) and never rambled on about my past glories.

I also never once pushed my children to become runners. My wife and I were both active people and we raised a very physically active family. We were always playing tag, throwing balls, running around in the very natural, happy way that kids enjoy. It wasn't too different from the street games my mother taught me to play back in the Bronx in the 50s and 60s.

When my oldest, Lauren, was a freshman in high school, I remember discouraging her from running cross country that first fall. "Why not play a sport that's more fun?" I asked her. She became a runner anyway and soon was showing that she had some special talent. At the same time, she was a very gifted violin player, and was on track to follow her classmates to a musical scholarship at Oberlin. But at a key juncture in high school, the two schedules conflicted and she had to choose between track and violin.

Frankly it pissed me off that a talented, motivated kid should have to choose between two things she loved. And neither her mother nor I pressured her in either direction. The only thing I offered was, "You should choose whatever you're more passionate about. All I can say is, I can personally help you a little more with running."

Lauren ended up choosing track, going All-American in the 1500 at the US Junior Nationals, won eight Maryland state titles in the 800, mile, and two-mile, and was two-time Maryland cross-country champion. So, by her junior year she was getting recruited by dozens of schools. Coaches and athletic directors from places like Princeton and Cornell were in our living room, wining and dining us. Lauren was impressively measured through this process, but I think the experience had just as much impact on her younger brother Matthew.

Throughout his boyhood Matthew loved nothing more than soccer. Watching it, playing FIFA with his friends, and playing it. I was usually busy with coaching and rarely attended his games, but I loved to see my son play a sport he loved. And he was very good at it. But what little I knew about soccer was that world-class talent is identified and cultivated very early, so by middle school it was pretty apparent what his ceiling was going to be. But there was nothing wrong with that.

I got myself in trouble once at the rare soccer game I attended when one of the parents was flying off the handle about this or that call and I said, "Listen buddy, none of these kids are going to be playing for Barcelona, okay? So chill out." The other soccer parents were so mad they made me stand on the far side of the field away from all the rest of them. I didn't mind this. In truth, I liked hiding out away from all the other parents. It reminded me of Bill Dellinger. At Oregon, whenever we wanted to find him at an important meet, whether it was the Pac 12 or National Championships, all we had to do was look for the place furthest away from the track and there was be a good chance he was sitting there watching the meet, stopwatch in hand. During meets, he never felt he needed to be on top of us. The "hay was in the barn" by then and there was little he could do to help us. I wanted to be the same way. I didn't want to be on top of my kids. If they needed me there that close, then I hadn't done my job as a parent.

When Matthew started high school, he played soccer in the fall and ran track in the spring. He immediately showed real potential as a distance runner, running a 9:47 in the 3200m as a freshman. And when he saw his sister Lauren headed off to Stanford on a full athletic scholarship, I could see the writing on the wall.

"Dad, I'm thinking of running cross country in the fall instead of playing soccer," he told me.

"You sure, Matthew?" I asked him—he was always Matthew in the family, and I was Matt. There was never any business about Sr. and Jr. "I don't think I ever saw a kid love anything as much as you love soccer."

"Coach Dobbs says I have the kind of talent to go really far," he said. Dana Dobbs was the track and cross-country coach. "What do you think?"

I shrugged. "Running is hard. For most people, it's not fun. If you can't find a way to love it, no matter how much natural potential you have, you won't excel. That's a question you have to ask yourself."

He nodded and then went up to his room. The next day he told me he decided he'd run cross country.

An interesting side note – as Lauren's success grew, so did her team's, and by the end of her high school career, her team would win back-to-back state cross country championships, a feat the team hadn't achieved before her arrival or duplicated since. In the same fashion, Mathew had a similar effect on his team, taking his Broadneck team from non-contenders to back-to-back state championships. It goes to show you – people gravitate towards championship people, towards winners. I don't know what that ingredient is, but champions raise the caliber of performance of everyone around them.

And, so, without an ounce of pressure from me—and I'm sure there are readers who won't believe me, but my kids will tell you it's true—I suddenly had two elite runners for children. As I said earlier, I don't think you can make a runner. A distance runner is someone that has to love to run, love to train and love to compete. It really takes a lot of self-motivation to train in the cold and rain, especially when one has to do it alone, and not as part of a team. It takes a kind of hardwired inner fire that to most people might seem borderline crazy.

My youngest daughter, Marisa, is a testament to my parenting style. Beverly and I raised her very similar to Lauren and Mathew – exposing her to all of the same things from the running world and the real world alike. We held her to the same standard – that regardless of where you choose to put your focus, you must excel. Ultimately, after running competititively as a freshman in high school, Marisa decided running was not for her. But she took the same winning principles and carved out her own path – graduating with honors from one of the nation's elite nursing programs at Drexel University.

**

Lauren was more successful at Stanford than I could have ever imagined. She was a five-time All-American and set the American Record as part of the 4x1500m relay. Lauren always brushed off my occasional forays into advice, so I let well enough alone. She had good coaches and was achieving great things. And just as importantly to me and her mother, she was thriving in the incredibly demanding academic environment of Stanford. They call it the Ivy of the West and they don't mess around when it comes to classes, even for top athletes.

Matthew on the other hand was not a natural student. He was incredibly smart but his motivation with his studies came and went. I always used to ask him, when he got a report card, "Any Cs?" He knew that Cs meant he would be grounded.

One day during his sophomore year I picked him up after cross-country practice on the day of his report card and asked the usual question, "Any Cs on there?"

"No, he said, no Cs."

"Good," I said, putting the car into gear. I was glad he was applying himself.

"But..." he said, "I did get two Ds."

I laughed. Funny kid. Takes after his old man. And then I glanced over and see Matthew's not laughing. He looks nervous as hell. He actually got two Ds.

My face goes cold and I drive him home, not saying a word for the rest of the ride. He knows he's in for it. When we get home I tell him to go out and rake the yard. I'm so furious that as soon as he has a full bag of leaves I stomp out there and grab the bag, throwing it around and spreading leaves all over the yard again.

"There," I said, "Rake it up again. I want you to remember how this feels. Because if you get those grades again this is what you're going to be doing for the rest of your life."

Was it excessive? I'll admit it probably was. But I'll tell you one thing: he never got another D again. I would like to add that I don't see anything wrong with people that do yard work for a living, or for that matter, the work of a housemaid. In fact, I especially admire those people. People like my mother, that gave an honest day's work for an honest day's pay. My real point to Matthew that day was that I wanted him to realize that he was lucky to be able to go to a good school, have a good home situation and that it was important that he work hard. Life's not easy, but if you work hard, you'll make the most of your opportunities.

***

Matthew continued to develop into a stellar runner, and his passion for it really grew. He didn't need to be told to keep up with his running log. It was always him peppering me with questions about the sport.

I remember in his sophomore year he read a local newspaper article about himself and saw a paragraph about his father. It referred to me as a "two-time Olympian." He was shocked. He honestly didn't know I had run in the Olympics. He'd thought— and I'd let him think—that I was a coach who ran a little bit in the old days but was nothing special. So, after this he's in my ear about everything. And of course as a coach, a father, and a former runner, I do what I can to help.

I tried to keep one principle that Dellinger taught me: don't give them everything at once. I'd keep Matthew's appetite whetted, leave him wanting more. Not overload him with every piece of knowledge I had all at once.

Soon he was calling me immediately after every race, even before his cool-down lap. (I could rarely attend his meets because of my own coaching schedule). But I'd always answer eagerly, excited to hear about his results. Unlike me, he had elite leg speed and could prove to be really special in the mile and 1500m.

His junior year at the Penn Relays—which luckily I could attend—I got to see my daughter set the American Record in the 6000m relay. Matthew was there as well, about to run the 3000m the next day. We were walking through the lobby together and saw a display of USA Track and Field gear. Matthew is standing there salivating over it, so I say "Tell you what, if you win, I'll get you one of the USA Sweatshirts."

He's wide-eyed, "Can you really do that?"

I have no idea. Suddenly my mind flashes back to Pete Squires stealing the whole box of T-shirts back in '73 in Spokane.

"I promise. I'll get you one." One of my parenting rules is never use the word "promise." I would always force myself to say "I'll try my best." Precise language is so important with kids. They

.arter and more perceptive than we give them credit for.

 in this case, I broke my own rule. I promised him. So, if he delivered on his end, I'd have to.

The next day he went out and destroyed the field with an 8:20.9.

After he wins the first thing he asks is about the sweatshirt. "So dad, are you going to get it?"

I said to him, "I promised I would. But there are two ways we can go about this. I can get you one. Or you can get it by making the junior national team."

It took him about two seconds to decide he wanted to earn it on his own. And he did.

That performance caught everyone's attention and suddenly Matthew was one of the most hotly recruited runners in the country. Georgetown, Michigan, Notre Dame, Stanford and Texas. And of course Oregon.

I helped Matthew narrow his choices down, offered my opinions on the coaches, the facilities, and the programs, but always emphasized the choice was his alone. Finally, he had it narrowed down to two choices: Texas or Oregon.

His visit to Texas was a master-class in recruitment. Coach Jason Vigilante did a brilliant job in wooing him, with every detail planned out. He even made sure that star runner Leo Manzano's locker was open when Matthew toured the locker room, so he could see the 10 pairs of Longhorn color custom Nikes that had Manzano's name monogrammed on them.

His visit to Oregon was strong as well, but less flashy. To a young kid, it was hard to ignore the flash. And maybe he'd be better off not running at my alma mater, not needing to worry about competing with his father's shadow. With the same exact name, I couldn't blame him for doing that.

His final question to me was: "If I hit a home run, where is the best place to be?"

I said, "Frankly, at the end of the day, Phil Knight cares most about one school: Oregon. If you turn out to be something special and want to hit the jackpot, Oregon is the place to be."

Without blinking he said, "Okay, Dad, I'm going to Oregon."

After he notified Oregon, I was concerned about Matthew losing some focus in the spring of his senior year. Like I did, 40-something years earlier, he had the opportunity to break 4 minutes as a high schooler. I knew how fast that window closed and I tried to keep him hungry.

I remember one race we were planning for him to run a 4:10 and he called me saying, "Dad I won the race. 4:12."

I said, "I don't care if you won. You're two seconds off your time. You know you can beat that."

A week later the goal was 4:04. He called me, "Okay, this time I hit 4:04."

I asked, "What were the tenths."

He laughed and said, "Flat."

***

Like me he didn't quite get below 4-minutes—his high school PR was 4:03.4--but he set the Maryland state record, and was clearly well on his way to being a better runner than I ever could have been at that distance. While I was too big from the jump in high school, he was slowly adding muscle to his frame over the four years—from literally 90 pounds as a freshman. Mathew ended his high school career with a National Championship in the 2 mile – running 8:41.5 to tie none other than Steve Prefontaine for 3rd on the all time high school list at that time.

By this point my hands-off approach early in his career had grown into a pretty intense one, and I'll be the first to admit it hurt him his first year at Oregon. He was a 17-year-old college freshman 3,000 miles away from home, so he was homesick from the start. I had the benefit of doing my first year at Manhattan just a couple of blocks from my friends and family.

And then he'd call me with reservations about the cross-country workouts he was doing. I never liked to second-guess another coach, but there were things I disagreed with. I tried not to say it, but I think he could tell in my tone. By the end of his fall season, he felt like he hadn't improved at all, and was talking about transferring.

He asked if I would be okay if he transferred to American University to run under me. That's when I knew I had to let go.

"No," I told him, "That won't be good for your development. And it wouldn't be good for our relationship as a father and son. You've got the best college coaches in the world at Oregon, the best facilities, and the best opportunities. Let me be more of a dad going forward and less of a coach. And you're going to do great."

And, entirely due to the effort of Matthew and his coaches, he did. In 2009, he ran a 3:59.3 split to help break the NCAA 4x mile record. That fall he made All-American—something I never achieved—in cross country. He was now on his way, as he continued to gain confidence and improve. In 2011 he won both the NCAA Championship and the National championship in the 1500m. Later that year, he made the USA World

Championship team in the 1500 and went on to win the bronze medal at the World Championships in South Korea. All of a sudden he was recognized as one of the best 1500 runners in the world. Feeling like there was nothing left to prove at the collegiate level, Matthew decided to turn pro and run for the Oregon Project under my old teammate Alberto Salazar. As part of turning professional, he also signed a big contract with Nike, which was great, but along with joining the Oregon Project and signing a major endorsement contract came real pressure to perform.

With Alberto as his coach, I tried to pull my presence as a coach back even further. Like Bill Dellinger did to me, so many years earlier, when I left Oregon—I wanted most of all to be Matthew's friend. He was now a professional runner, working under one of the best coaches in the world. He didn't need my coaching advice, but I do think he needed me to be his friend and his father.

The next year, 2012, was an Olympic year. Since he had won the bronze in the World Championships the year before, he had an enormous amount of pressure on him. Everybody automatically assumed he should medal at the London Olympic Games. Like I said before, it was time for me to be both a father and a friend. The counsel I offered him at this point was as a former runner more than a coach. I had been to two Olympic Trials and knew the unique stresses. I'd been to the Olympic Games and knew all too well how dazzling and distracting everything could be. For Matthew, it was especially tough, as just a couple of months before the Olympics, he was suffering from an injury. I cannot stress enough how worrisome it is for an athlete to deal with the uncertainty of an injury just weeks before the Olympic Trials.

I offered two pieces of advice to him. First, as he made his final preparations for London, I told him to communicate clearly with Alberto. Alberto by this point was of course a god of coaching. He was legendary, he had an aura. At the start Matthew was so intimidated by him, he hesitated to say anything that might be construed as pushing back. I told him, "Alberto wants to hear how you're feeling. These workouts are customized for you. For him to design your training to its best potential, he needs to know when they aren't going well, as much as when they are."

The second important piece of advice I gave him came after the Olympic final. He ran a terrific race, especially for a kid running his first Olympic final, but he came up short. He finished fourth in London, missing bronze by a mere .04 seconds. That night I arrived at a dinner where his friends and teammates were going to meet him and it was like a funeral. I went crazy. I went off on everybody, "You think 4th in the

191

Olympic Games is something to be sad about? I don't want to see a single sad face in here." Matthew needed to know that what he had accomplished was great and that he should have been proud and happy.

He and his friends understood, and pepped up. When Matthew showed up a few minutes later he was touched to see everybody in a good mood, toasting his very real accomplishment. But I could tell when we were back inside that he was in real pain. After about an hour he stepped outside with me to talk and then bawled his eyes out. Seeing that hurt worse than any loss I ever took as a runner. However, I also knew my boy had the heart of a champion.

I never got a second Olympics. I hoped in my heart—and knew in my gut that night that he would.

THE HOME STRETCH

The ridiculously slow pace of the first two laps gave way to anxious tension. Everybody in the stadium was ready for an extremely fast finish. I strapped my seat belt on and was running with Matthew from that point on.

At about 500m from the finish, Ayanleh Souleiman burst in front of Matthew, but was unable to pull far enough out to cut inside to the rail, leaving him dangerously situated on the outside at the upcoming turn which would feed him additional ground to cover in that place. I knew Matthew loved running people wide, and there was no way this late he was going to surrender the rail. He settled the matter twenty meters later with a short burst and managed to squeeze ahead of Souleiman by passing him just inside the rail, giving him a subtle nudge with his elbow.

Souleiman, who had already run the 800 and was probably the runner most disrupted by Kemoi's earlier fall, seemed to wilt at Matthew's power move. When Matthew made that decisive move, I could sense his confidence up in the stands.

And now they were at the final lap. The final 400 meters that would separate the legends from the merely great. Did Kiprop have Matthew's number? Could he uncork that miraculous long stride of his to defeat the blistering final 400 I knew Matthew was ready to unleash?

If the third lap picked the pace up, the fourth one rocketed it. As unusually slow the first 800 had been, this final 400 was going to be one of the fastest ever. Matthew's God-given leg-speed, years of training, and mental toughness kicked into overdrive.

The long-dreaded kick by Kiprop came on the backstretch. Relaxed and graceful, Kiprop seemed to just float past runner after runner until he was right on Matthew's shoulder. I'd say they ran stride for stride, but nobody could run as fast as Kiprop with so few steps. But the turn was coming and Kiprop was still unable to get past Matthew.

My jaw dropped when they hit turn starting the final 200. He's got it. He'll run them all wide.

Kiprop's face said that he knew it too. His tank was on E—if he couldn't take Matthew in that back straightaway there was no way he'd outsprint him in the final 100 meters. Kiprop faded.

194

Matthew ran Makhloufi out wide. He held on. He did it. Finish line.

Gold. Medal.

It all came out. Everything. My love for my son. The pain of my own near misses at running immortality. The anguish of growing up fatherless. The insanely hard work I saw he put in and the discipline he had that I never possessed. All of it was there, all at once.

I watch the video of myself at that finish and almost don't recognize myself. My daughter Lauren beside me and friends who've seen Matthew grow up around me, I completely lost it. People back home told me that watching us at the close of Matthew's race was like nothing else they had seen during NBC's coverage of the entire Rio Olympics. No, we weren't the polite family and friends clapping and cheering for our loved one. No, I was Matt, the kid from the Bronx, going crazy, my daughter crying, my friends body surfing over each other like little kids. It didn't cross anyone's mind for a second that we were being watched by millions of people around the world. We were just enjoying the moment, and what a moment it was.

Matthew, as usual, had more poise.

The American flag now draped on his shoulders, he ran up to my section of the stands. I knew the camera would be on me, but I couldn't help myself. "Are you f***ing kidding me!?" I yelled. (Sorry, NBC)

This really happened. He led from start to finish. He finished with an unreal final 400 in 50.62 in the final 400 meters. He had taken what some of the best runners in history had to dish out and he conquered them. The race that had haunted Americans for over a century, the race that thwarted greats like Jim Ryun, Marty Liquori, Steve Scott and Alan Webbhad been conquered by my own son. Until that day, no American runner had won the Olympic 1500 since Teddy Roosevelt was in office in 1908.

That night I didn't touch a drink. I didn't want to forget a second of it. I stayed that night in the same room with Matthew. Still buzzing from the frenzy of the last 24 hours, I had trouble falling asleep. I looked over to Matthew lying still in his bed.

"son, you awake?" I ask him softly.

He perks up, "yeah, Dad, what's up?" he replies, rolling over to face me.

"My son, Olympic champion, I still can't believe this is real..."

Reaching under his pillow, he pulls out the gold medal. "Me neither, Dad!" grinning as the medal swings from his hand.

I know it won't last forever. All we can do is enjoy it.

Made in the USA
Middletown, DE
10 May 2017